Stories Of The Italian Artists From Vasari

ANGELS. By ORCAGNA.

STORIES

OF THE

ITALIAN ARTISTS

FROM VASARI

NEW YORK
HENRY MILFORD

STORIES

OF THE

ITALIAN ARTISTS

From *VASARI*, G.

BY THE
AUTHOR OF "*BELT AND SPUR*," ETC.

With Sixteen Illustrations

Then in the Thirteenth Century men wake as if
they heard an alarum through the whole vault of
heaven, and true human life begins again; and the
cradle of this life is the Val d'Arno.

J. RUSKIN, *Ariadne Florentina.*

NEW YORK
SCRIBNER & WELFORD
1885

PREFACE.

THE title of this book seems to me to describe its
contents so clearly that there will be no need to say
much in explanation of its purport. I have tried in
these stories to give an idea of the liveliness of the
Renaissance in Italy and of that exuberant enjoy-
ment of the revived arts, which finds such vivid
expression in the pages of Vasari. That he is often
incorrect has of course been discovered long since.
As he himself said, " If writers of history were to
live somewhat longer than is usually granted to the
course of human life, they would often have to alter
the things written by them ; for as it is not possible
that one man, however diligent he may be, should in
so short a time discover all the truth, so it is as
clear as the sun that Time, who is called the father
of truth, will daily discover to students new things."
As this book, however, has no pretensions to be a
critical work, I have simply followed Vasari, and tell
the tales as nearly as I can in his own words. His

treatment of Raphael has been attributed to pre-
judice, and indeed he was such a devoted disciple of
Michael Angelo, and so vain of his intimacy with
the great man, that his judgment could scarcely be
unbiassed. Many great names will be missed here,
for Vasari's account is often confined to a bare
description of the painter's works with a meagre
outline of his life; and it must not be forgotten that
he did not carry on his history to the later painters,
such as Tintoretto and Veronese.

CONTENTS.

LIST OF ILLUSTRATIONS.

STORIES FROM VASARI.

CHAPTER I.

CIMABUE AND GIOTTO.

THE great deluge of evils which had overthrown and afflicted poor Italy, had not only ruined all buildings worthy of the name, but what was of more importance, had exhausted all the artists, when in the year 1240, by the will of God, there was born in the city of Florence, Giovanni, surnamed Cimabue, of the noble family of that name, who was to shed the first light on the art of painting. He, as he grew, being judged by his father and others to possess a fine acute intellect, was sent to S. Maria Novella to be instructed in letters by a relative of his who taught grammar to the novices of that convent. But Cimabue, instead of attending to his lessons, spent all the day in painting on his books and papers, men, horses, houses, and such things. To this natural inclination fortune was favourable, for some painters of Greece, who had been summoned by the rulers of

2

Florence to restore the almost forgotten art of painting in the city, began to work in the chapel of the Gondi in S. Maria Novella ; and Cimabue would often escape from school and stand all day watching them, until his father and the painters themselves judging that he was apt for painting, he was placed under their instruction.   Nature, however, aided by constant practice, enabled him greatly to surpass both in design and colouring the masters who had taught him.   For they, never caring to advance, did everything not in the good manner of ancient Greece, but after the rude manner of those times.

He painted in churches both in Florence and Pisa, making the name of Cimabue famous everywhere, on which account he was summoned to Assisi, a city of Umbria, to paint in company with some Greek masters the lower church of S. Francis.   For in those times the order of the Minor Friars of S. Francis having been confirmed by Pope Innocent III., both the devotion and the numbers of the friars grew so great not only in Italy, but in all parts of the world, that there was scarcely a city of any account which did not build for them churches and convents at great expense.   Two years before the death of S. Francis, while that saint was absent preaching, Fra Elià was prior in Assisi, and built a church for our Lady; but when S. Francis was dead, and all Christendom was coming to visit the body of a saint who in life and death was known by all to have been

the friend of God, every man at the holy spot making
gifts according to his power, it was ordained that the
church begun by Fra Elià should be made much
larger and more magnificent. But there being a
scarcity of good architects, and the work needing an
excellent one, for it was necessary to build on a very
steep hill at the roots of which runs a torrent called
Tescio, they brought to Assisi after much consideration, as the best that could then be found, one
Master Jacopo Tedesco. He having considered the
site, and heard the will of the Fathers, who held a
chapter-general for the purpose in Assisi, designed a
very fine church and convent, making in the model
three storeys, one below ground, and the others for
two churches, one of which on the first slope should
serve as the vestibule, having a very large colonnade
round it, and the other for the sanctuary. And he
arranged that you should go up from the first to the
second by a most convenient order of stairs, which
wound round the larger chapel, dividing into two, to
enter the second church. To this he gave the form
of a T, making it five times as long as it was wide.
In the larger chapel of the lower church was placed
the altar, and below it, when it was finished, was
laid with solemn ceremonies the body of S. Francis.
And because the tomb which encloses the body of the
glorious saint is in the first, that is the lowest church,
which no one ever enters, the doors of it are
walled up, and around the altar are gratings of iron,

with rich ornaments of marble and mosaic. This work was brought to a conclusion in the space of four years, and no more, by the skill of Master Jacopo and the careful labours of Fra Èlià. After his death there were made round the lower church twelve fine towers, and in each of them a staircase from the ground to the top, and in time there were added many chapels and many rich ornaments. As for Master Jacopo, by this work he acquired such fame through all Italy that he was called to Florence, and received there with the greatest honour possible, although, according to the habit the Florentines have (and used to have still more) of shortening names, they called him not Jacopo but Lapo all the days of his life.

So Cimabue painted in company with the Greeks in the lower church, and greatly surpassed the Greek painters. Therefore, his courage rising, he began to paint by himself in fresco in the upper church, and painted many things, especially the ascent of the Virgin into heaven, and the Holy Spirit descending upon the apostles. This work, being truly very great and rich and well executed, must in my judgment having astonished the world in those days, painting having been so long in such darkness, and to myself, who saw it in the year 1563, it appeared most beautiful, and I marvelled how Cimabue could have had such light in the midst of such heavy gloom. Being called to Florence, however, Cimabue did not continue his labours, but they were finished many years after by Giotto, as we will tell in its place.

After his return to Florence he made for the church of S. Maria Novella a picture of our Lady, which work was of larger size than those that had been made before that time, and the angels that stand round, although they are in the Greek manner, yet show something of the modern style. Therefore this work caused such marvel to the people of that time, never having seen a better, that it was borne in solemn procession with trumpets and great rejoicing from the house of Cimabue to the church, and he himself received great honours and rewards. It is said, and you may read it in certain records of old pictures, that while Cimabue was painting this picture, King Charles of Anjou passed through Florence, and among other entertainments provided for him by the people of the city, they took him to see Cimabue's picture, and as no one had seen it before it was shown to the king, there was a great concourse of all the men and women of Florence to see it, with the greatest rejoicing and running together in the world. From the gladness of the whole neighbourhood that part was called Borgo-Allegri, the Joyful Quarter, and though it is now within the walls of the city, it has always preserved the same name.

Now in the country of Florence, about fourteen

miles from the city, in the village of Vespignano,
there was born to a simple peasant named Bondone,
in the year 1276, a son to whom he gave the name
of Giotto, and whom he brought up according to his
station. And when he had reached the age of ten
years, showing in all his ways though still childish
an extraordinary vivacity and quickness of mind,
which made him beloved not only by his father but
by all who knew him, Bondone gave him the care of
some sheep. And he leading them for pasture, now
to one spot and now to another, was constantly
driven by his natural inclination to draw on the
stones or the ground some object in nature, or something that came into his mind. One day Cimabue,
going on business from Florence to Vespignano,
found Giotto, while his sheep were feeding, drawing
a sheep from nature upon a smooth and solid rock
with a pointed stone, having never learnt from any
one but nature. Cimabue, marvelling at him, stopped
and asked him if he would go and be with him.
And the boy answered that if his father were content
he would gladly go. Then Cimabue asked Bondone
for him, and he gave him up to him, and was content
that he should take him to Florence. There in a
little time, by the aid of nature and the teaching of
Cimabue, the boy not only equalled his master, but
freed himself from the rude manner of the Greeks,
and revived the good art of painting, introducing the
drawing from nature of living persons, which had not

been practised for two hundred years; or at least if some had tried it, they had not succeeded very happily. Giotto painted among others, as may be seen to this day in the chapel of the Podestà's Palace at Florence, Dante Alighieri, his contemporary and great friend, and no less famous a poet than Giotto was a painter.

Afterwards he was called to Assisi by Fra Giovanni di Muro, at that time general of the order of S. Francis, and painted in fresco in the upper church thirty-two stories from the life and deeds of S. Francis, which brought him great fame. It is no wonder therefore that Pope Benedict sent one of his courtiers into Tuscany to see what sort of a man he was and what his works were like, for the Pope was planning to have some paintings made in S. Peter's. This courtier, on his way to see Giotto and to find out what other masters of painting and mosaic there were in Florence, spoke with many masters in Sienna, and having received some drawings from them, he came to Florence. And one morning going into the workshop of Giotto, who was at his labours, he showed him the mind of the Pope, and at last asked him to give him a little drawing to send to his Holiness. Giotto, who was a man of courteous manners, immediately took a sheet of paper, and with a pen dipped in red, fixing his arm firmly against his side to make a compass of it, with a turn of his hand he made a circle so perfect that it was a marvel to see it. Having done it, he turned smiling to the courtier and said, " Here is the .drawing." But he, thinking he was being laughed at, asked, " Am I to have no other drawing than this ? " " This is enough and too much," replied Giotto, " send it with the others and see if it will be understood." The messenger, seeing that he could get nothing else, departed ill pleased, not doubting that he had been made a fool of. However, sending the other drawings to the Pope with the names of those who had made them, he sent also Giotto's, relating how he had made the circle without moving his ·arm and without compasses, which when the Pope and many of his courtiers understood, they saw that Giotto must surpass greatly all the other painters of his time. This thing being told, there arose from it a proverb which is still used about men of coarse clay, " You are rounder than the O of Giotto," which proverb is not only good because of the occasion from which it sprang, but also still more for its significance, which consists in its ambiguity, *tondo*, " round," meaning in Tuscany not only a perfect circle, but also slowness and heaviness of mind.

So the Pope made him come to Rome, and he painted for him in S. Peter's, and there never left his hands work better finished ; wherefore the Pope, esteeming himself well served, gave him six hundred ducats of gold, besides having shown him so many favours that it was spoken of through all Italy.

TWO APOSTLES. By GIOTTO.

After Giotto was returned to Florence, Robert, king of Naples, wrote to his eldest son, Charles, king of Calabria, who was at that time in Florence, that he must by some means or other send him Giotto to Naples. Giotto hearing himself called by a king so famous and so much praised, went very willingly to serve him, and did many works which pleased the king greatly. And he was so much beloved by him that the king would often visit him, and took pleasure in watching him work and listening to his conversation, and Giotto, who had always some jest or some witty answer ready, would converse with him while going on with his painting. So one day the king saying to him that he would make him the first man in Naples, Giotto answered, "And that is why I am lodged at the Porta Reale, that I may be the first man in Naples." And another time the king saying to him, "Giotto, if I were you, now that it is hot, I would give up painting a little," he answered, "And so would I, certainly, if I were you."

So pleasing the king well, he painted him a good number of pictures, and the portraits of many famous men, Giotto himself among them; and one day the king, as a caprice, asked him to paint his kingdom. Giotto, it is said, painted a laden ass with a new load lying at his feet, which while it refused it seemed to desire, and both on the new and old burden was the royal crown and sceptre of power. And when Giotto was asked by the king what the

picture signified, he replied, " Such must be the
subjects and such the kingdom which every day
desired a new lord."

There are many other stories remaining of the
witty sayings of Giotto, and besides those that are
told by Boccaçcio, Franco Sacchetti tells many good
ones, some of which I will give in Franco's own words.

" How a man of little station gives Giotto the
great painter a shield to paint.

" Every one must have heard of Giotto, who was
a great painter above any other. A rough workman,
hearing of his fame, came to Giotto's workshop
followed by one carrying his shield. Arrived there,
he found Giotto, and said, ' God save you, master, I
want you to paint my arms on this shield.' Giotto,
considering the man and his manner of speech, said
nothing but, ' When do you want it ? ' And he told
him. Giotto said, ' Leave me to do it ; ' so he went
away. And Giotto, left alone, said to himself, ' What
did he mean ? Has some sent him for a joke ? I
never had a shield to paint before. And this man
was a simple fellow, and bade me paint his arms as
if he were of the royal house of France. Certainly
I shall have to make him some new arms.' So
thinking to himself, he put the shield before him
and made a design and bade one of his pupils paint
it, and so it was done. There was a helmet, a
gorget, a pair of iron gloves, a cuirass, and cuisses,
a sword, dagger, and lance. So the worthy man

came again and said, 'Master, is my shield painted?'
Giotto answered, 'Certainly, bring it down.' But
when it came the would-be gentleman looked at it
and said, 'What is this you have been painting? I
won't pay four farthings for it.' Giotto said, 'What
did you tell me to paint?' And he answered, 'My
arms.' 'Are not they all here?' asked Giotto;
'what is wanting? Nay, you are a great fool, for if
any one were to ask you who you are, you would
hardly know what to answer; and you come here
and say, Paint me my arms. What arms do you
bear? Whence are you? Who were your ancestors?
I have painted all your armour on the shield, and if
there is anything else, tell me and I will add it.'
But the other answered, 'You are giving me vile
words, and have spoilt my shield.' And he went
away and summoned Giotto before the justice.
Giotto appeared, and on his side summoned him,
demanding two florins for his painting. And when
the court had heard the matter, they gave sentence
that the man should take his shield so painted, and
pay six lire to Giotto."

It is said that when Giotto was only a boy with
Cimabue, he once painted a fly on the nose of a face
that Cimabue had drawn, so naturally that the
master returning to his work tried more than once to
drive it away with his hand, thinking it was real.
And I might tell you of many other jests played by
Giotto, but of this enough.

CHAPTER II.

AMONG the old painters who were much alarmed by
the praises so deservedly bestowed upon Cimabue
and Giotto was one Margaritone, a painter of Arezzo,
who having held a high rank among those who
practised the art in that unhappy age became aware
that the works of these new men would almost
entirely eclipse his fame. He had been considered
excellent by the other painters of his time who
worked in the old Greek style, and had painted
many pictures in Arezzo, both in tempera and fresco.
For the church of S. Margherita he painted a work
on canvas stretched on a panel, in which are many
pictures containing little figures representing stories
from the lives of our Lady and the saints; and the
picture is noteworthy not only because the little
figures are painted so well that they seem to be
miniatures, but also because it is a marvel to see a
work on canvas that has been preserved three
hundred years. He made a great number of pictures

CHAPTER II

AGATTI AND ... PTALMACCO.

... were much alarmed by
... might bestowed upon Christian
a ... a painter of ...,
who have ... rank among those who
... happy ... are aware
that ... k ... new men ... almost
... like ... He ... murdered
by the ... of the time who
... say, and had painted
... repented ...
... he ... paint ... a work
... a work, in which are many
... the ...; and the
... very because the had
... they ... to be
... it is a marvel to see a
... ast ... been painted there ...
He ... an ... number of pictures

APPEARANCE OF S. NICHOLAS. **By** MARGARITONE.

all over the city, and having painted on wood a large
crucifix in the Greek style, he sent it to Florence to
the famous citizen Farinata degli Uberti, because he
had, among his other great works, saved his country
from danger and ruin. Afterwards he gave himself
to sculpture with so much application that he succeeded much better than he had in painting. He
died at the age of seventy-seven, disgusted, it is said,
with life, because he had seen the age change so
much and new artists obtain honour.

Andrea Tafi for his works in mosaic was greatly
admired, and he himself considered almost divine ;
but Gaddo the Florentine, who worked with him at
Pisa, showed more knowledge of design, and perhaps this arose from his friendship with Cimabue.
For either through conformity of nature or the goodness of their hearts, they were united in a close
attachment, and while discoursing lovingly together
over the difficulties of their art, the noblest and
greatest conceptions were ever in their minds. And
this so much the more because they were aided by
the subtle air of Florence, which is wont to produce
ingenious and subtle spirits. For those who study
any science by conferring together clear it and make
it more easy. But some on the contrary have
wickedly made a profession of friendship with specious
appearance of love, only in malice and envy to de-
fraud others of their conceptions. But true love
bound together Gaddo and Cimabue, and also Andrea

Tafi and Gaddo. Andrea took him to aid him in the
mosaics of S. Giovanni, and afterwards he worked
alone and applied himself to the study of the Greek
manner, together with that of Cimabue. So his
fame being spread abroad, he was called to Rome
and to other cities. Afterwards returning to Florence
for rest after his labours, he set himself to making
little tablets of mosaic, some of which he made of
egg-shells, with incredible patience and diligence.
He painted also many pictures maintaining his reputation, but because the manner of painting in those
times cannot greatly help artists, I will pass them
over in silence. Gaddo lived seventy-three years,
dying in 1312, and was honourably buried in S.
Croce by Taddeo his son, and although he had many
sons, Taddeo, who had been held at the font by
Giotto, alone applied himself to painting, learning
the rudiments from his father and the rest from
Giotto, who was his master four and twenty years.
He, surpassing his fellow scholars, produced his first
works with a facility given him by nature rather
than by art. He was indeed an imitator of Giotto's
manner, whom he always held in the greatest veneration.

At the command of the commune he continued
the building of Orsanmichele, begun by Arnolfo di
Lapo, and repaired the pillars of the loggia, building
them of well-hewn stone where they had first been
made of brick, yet without altering the design that

Arnolfo di Lapo had left with the intention that over the loggia should be a palace of two storeys, for storing the grain of the people and commune of Florence. And that the work might be finished, the Guild of S. Maria, which had the charge of the building, gave orders that the tax on the sale of grain and other little customs should go towards it. But what was of more importance, it was ordained with great wisdom that each of the guilds of Florence should make a pillar and set up in a niche in it the patron saint of the guild, and every year on the feast-day the consuls of the guild should go there for offerings, setting up their standard and standing by the pillar the whole day, but the offerings given to the Madonna should still be for the help of those in need.

In the year 1333 a great flood of waters swept away the defences of the bridge Rubaconte, over-threw the castle Altafronte, and left nothing of the old bridge but the two middle piers. The bridge of the Holy Trinity was altogether destroyed except one pier, which was left in a shattered state; and half the bridge at Carraja was swept away, the sluices of Ogni Santi bursting. So those who had the rule of the city deliberated upon this matter, and not being willing that those who lived on the other side of the Arno should be placed in such discomfort as to have to pass to and from their houses by boats, they called for Taddeo Gaddo and bade him make a model and

design for rebuilding the old bridge, charging him
to make it as handsome and fine as could be. He
therefore, sparing neither expense nor trouble, built
it with great piers and with magnificent arches of
hewn stone, so that to this day it bears the weight
of twenty-two shops on each side, in all forty-four,
to the great advantage of the commune, which
receives from them every year eight hundred florins
for rent. For this work, which cost sixty thousand
gold florins, Taddeo deserved infinite praise then,
and is more to be commended now than ever, for,
not to speak of other floods, it remained unmoved
on the 13th day of September, 1537, when the water
brought down the bridge of the Holy Trinity, two
arches of the Carraja bridge, ruined a great part of
the Rubaconte, besides doing other notable damage.
And indeed no one of any judgment can fail to
be astonished and to marvel that this old bridge
should have sustained unmoved the shock of the
water, the drift wood and the ruins swept down from
above.

Taddeo however did not cease from painting, and
made a great number of pictures of importance both
in Florence and elsewhere; and in process of time
he gained so much wealth that he laid the founda-
tion of the riches and nobility of the family, being
always held to be a wise man and prudent. He
painted the chapter-house of S. Maria Novella,
being called to the work by the prior of the place.

But because the work was great, and the chapter-house of Santo Spirito had been by that time uncovered, to the great fame of Simone Memmi who had painted it, the prior desired to give Simone half of the work, and conferring with Taddeo about it, found him right content, for he loved Simone greatly, they having been schoolfellows together under Giotto, and ever loving friends and companions. Oh, truly noble souls! without emulation or envy, loving one another like brothers, and rejoicing each one at the honour and praise of the other, as if it were his own! So the work was divided between them, three sides being given to Simone, and to Taddeo the left side and all the ceiling.

So Taddeo, having procured to himself by his industry and labours not only a name but also great riches, passed to the other life, leaving behind him his sons Agnolo and Giovanni, and hoping that Agnolo particularly would become excellent in painting. But he who in his youth showed signs of far surpassing his father, did not succeed according to the opinion that had been conceived of him, for having been born and brought up in ease, which has often proved an impediment to study, he gave himself more to traffic and merchandize than to the art of painting, which thing should not be thought either new or strange, for avarice has often hindered many who would have risen to great heights if the desire of gain in their

first and better years had not impeded their way.
Nevertheless he worked as the caprice took him,
sometimes with more care and sometimes with less,
and having in a sense inherited the secret of working in mosaic, having also in his house the instru-
ments and other things that Gaddo his grandfather
had used, he for pastime, when it seemed good to
him, made some things in mosaic. Thus many of
his works may be seen in Florence, at which he
laboured much to his own profit, though he worked
rather for the sake of doing as his fathers had done
than for the love of it, his mind going after merchandize, and when his sons, refusing to be painters, gave
themselves up wholly to trade, establishing a house
at Venice in partnership with their father, he worked
no more at his art, except for his pleasure.

Buonamico di Cristofano, nicknamed Buffalmacco,
was a pupil of Andrea Tafi, and has been celebrated
as a jester by Boccaccio. Franco Sacchetti also
tells how when Buffalmacco was still a boy with
Andrea, his master had the habit, when the nights
were long, of getting up before day to work, and calling his boys. This was displeasing to Buonamico,
who had to rise in the middle of his best sleep, and
he considered how he might prevent Andrea from
getting up before day to work, and this was what
occurred to him. Having found thirty great beetles in
an ill-kept cellar, he fastened on each of their backs
a little candle, and at the hour when Andrea was

used to rise, he put them one by one through a hole in the door into Andrea's chamber, having first lighted the candles. His master awaking, the time being come to call Buffalmacco, and seeing the lights, was seized with terror and began to tremble, like a fearful old man as he was, and to recommend his soul to heaven, and say his prayers, and repeat the psalms, and at last, putting his head under the clothes, he thought no more that night of calling Buffalmacco, but lay trembling with fear till daybreak. The morning being come, he asked Buonamico if, like him, he had seen more than a thousand demons. To which Buonamico answered no, for he had kept his eyes closed and wondered he had not been called. "What!" said Tafi, "I had something else to think of than painting, and I am resolved to go into some other house." The next night, although Buonamico only put three beetles into Tafi's chamber, yet he from the last night's terror and the fear of these few demons, could get no sleep at all, and as soon as it was day left the house determined never to return, and it took a great deal of good counsel to make him change his mind. At last Buonamico brought the priest to him to console him. And Tafi and Buonamico, discussing the matter, Buonamico said, "I have always heard say that demons are the greatest enemies of God, and consequently they ought to be the chief adversaries of painters, because not only do we always

make them hideous, but we also never cease making
saints on all the walls, and so cause men in despite
of the demons to become better and more devout.
So these demons being enraged against us, as they
have greater power by night than by day, they come
playing us these tricks, and it will be worse if this
custom of getting up early is not quite given up.'"
With such words Buffalmacco managed the matter,
what the priest said helping him, so that Tafi left
off getting up early, and the demons left off going
about the house at night with candles. But not
many months after, Tafi, drawn by the desire of
gain, and having forgotten his fears, began afresh to
get up early and to call Buffalmacco, whereupon the
beetles began again to appear, until he was forced
by his fears to give it up entirely, being earnestly
counselled to do so by the priest. And the matter
being noised abroad in the city for a time, neither
Tafi nor any other painter ventured to get up at
night to work.

But after a time Buffalmacco, having become a
good master himself, left Tafi, as Franco relates, and
began to work for himself, work never failing him.
Now he had taken a house both to work and to live
in next to a worker in wool, very well to do, who was
nicknamed Capodoca (Goosehead), and this man's
wife used to rise at daybreak just when Buffalmacco,
having worked till then, was going to rest. Sitting
down to her spinning-wheel, which by ill fortune was

just behind Buffalmacco's bed, she would set to work
to spin the yarn. So Buffalmacco, not being able to
sleep, began to think what he could do to remedy the
evil. And before long he perceived that, on the other
side of the wall of brick which divided him from
Capodoca, was the chimney of his neighbour, and
that through a hole he could see all that she did at
the fire. So having considered his trick, he hollowed
out a tube, and whenever Capodoca's wife was not
at the fire, through the hole in the wall he would
put as much salt as he liked into his neighbour's
saucepan. Capodoca then, coming home to his
dinner or supper, found many times that he could
eat neither soup nor meat, because everything was
too salt. Once or twice he was patient and only
grumbled a little, but when he found words were
not enough, several times he gave blows to the
poor woman, who was in despair, for she thougbt
herself very careful about seasoning her cookery.
And once when her husband beat her, she began
to excuse herself, which making Capodoca more
angry, he set to work again until she began to cry
as loud as she could, and all the neighbours ran to
see what was the matter. Among the rest came
Buffalmacco, and hearing of what Capodoca accused
his wife, and how she excused herself, he said to
Capodoca, " In faith, comrade, do you think you
are reasonable? You complain that morning and
evening your food is too salt, but I wonder how

your good woman does anything right. I don't
know how she keeps on her feet, considering that
all night she is at her spinning-wheel, and does
not sleep an hour, I believe. Stop her getting up
at midnight, and you will see that when she has
her fill of sleep her brains will be clear and she
will run into no more such errors." And turning
to the other neighbours, he put the matter before
them, so that they all said that Buonamico said
the truth, and he had better do as he advised. And
he believing that it was so, commanded her not to
get up so early. So the food was found to be reasonably salt, unless the woman got up early, when
Buffalmacco returned to his remedy, and Capodoca
made her give it up.

Among the first works that Buffalmacco undertook
was the painting of the church of the convent of
Faenza in Florence, and among other stories was
the slaughter of the Innocents by Herod, in which
he represented in a most lively manner the emotions
both of the slayers and the other figures, some of the
nurses and mothers tearing their children out of the
murderers' hands, and helping themselves as best
they could with their hands and their nails and
their teeth, and showing themselves as full of rage
and fury as of grief.

While doing this work for the ladies of Faenza,
Buffalmacco, who was very careless and negligent in
his dress as in other things, did not always wear his

hood and mantle as was the fashion at the time, and
the nuns, watching him through the screen he had
erected, began to complain that it did not please them
to see him in his doublet. At last, as he always appeared in the same fashion, they began to think that
he was only some boy employed in mixing colours,
and they gave him to understand through their
abbess that they should prefer to see his master and
not always him. To this Buonamico answered
good humouredly that when the master came he
would let them know, understanding nevertheless
how little confidence they had in him. Then he
took a stool and placed it upon another, and on the
top he put a pitcher or water-jug and fastened a
hood on the handle, and covered up the rest of the
jug with a cloak, fastening it well behind the tables,
and having fixed a pencil in the spout of the jug, he
went away. The nuns coming again to see the
picture through a hole that they had made in the
screen, saw the supposed master in his fine attire,
and not doubting that he was working with all his
might, doing very different work from what that boy
did, for several days were quite content. At last,
being desirous to see what fine things the master
had done in the last fortnight (during which time
Buonamico had not been there at all), one night,
thinking the master was gone, they went to see his
picture, and were overcome with confusion, when one
more bold than the rest detected the solemn master

who during the fortnight had done no work at all.
But acknowledging that he had only treated them
as they deserved, and that the work which he had
done was worthy of praise, they sent their steward
to call Buonamico back, and he with great laughter
went back to his work, letting them see the difference
between men and water-jugs, and that it does not do
always to judge a man's work by his clothes. So
in a few days he finished a picture with which they
were greatly pleased, except that the faces seemed to
them too pale and wan. Buonamico having heard
this, and knowing that the abbess had some wine
which was the best in Florence, and which she kept
for the mass, told them that if they wished to remedy
the defect it could only be done by mixing the colours
with good wine, and then if the cheeks were touched
with the colour they would become red and of a more
lively colour. The good sisters hearing this, and
ready to believe everything, kept him always supplied
with excellent wine while he worked, and he, while
enjoying the wine himself, to please them made his
colours more fresh and bright.

It is said that in 1302 he was fetched to Assisi,
and in the church of S. Francis painted the chapel
of S. Catherine with her history. When passing
through Arezzo after finishing the chapel, he was
stopped by the Bishop Guido, who having heard that
he was a pleasant man and a painter of worth,
desired him to paint the chapel in his house.

Buonamico set to work, and had already done a
great part when there befel him the strangest accident in the world, according to Franco Sacchetti.
The bishop had a monkey the most amusing and the
most mischievous that ever was seen. This animal
being sometimes on the scaffold watching Buonamico
work, gave his whole mind to the matter, and never
took his eyes off him when he was mixing his colours,
handling his paintpots, beating up the eggs to make
the tempera, or in fact doing any part of his work.
Now Buonamico left his work one Saturday evening,
and on Sunday morning this monkey, in spite of a
great log of wood which the bishop had had tied to
his feet to prevent his jumping about everywhere,
climbed on to the scaffold where he was used to sit
and watch Buonamico work, and having got hold of
the paintpots, poured their contents one into the
other and made up a mixture, breaking up all the eggs
there were, and began to paint with the brushes, and
never stopped until he had repainted everything.
This done he mixed up again all the colour that was
left, though that was little, and came down from the
scaffold and went away. So on Monday morning
Buonamico returned to his work, and finding the
painting spoilt, and the paintpots in a mess, and
everything wrong side upwards, he was thrown into
great confusion and dismay. But having considered
the matter well, he came to the conclusion that it
was some native of Arezzo who had done it out of

envy or some other reason ; therefore going to the
bishop, he told him what had happened and what he
supposed. The bishop was greatly troubled, but he
encouraged Buonamico to set to work again, and re-
paint what had been spoiled. And because he thought
what he suspected was very likely true, he gave him
six of his armed soldiers with orders to lie in wait with
their swords drawn whenever he was not working,
and to cut down without mercy any one who came.
So he painted it over a second time, and one day
when the soldiers were on guard they heard a noise
in the church, and behold in a moment the monkey
sprang on the scaffold, and the new master set to
work upon Buonamico's saints. So they called him
and showed him the malefactor, and stood watching him, all bursting with laughter, Buonamico
especially, who could not help laughing till he cried.
At last, dismissing the soldiers from their guard, he
went himself to the bishop and said, "My lord,
you want the painting done one way, and your
monkey wants it another." And having told him
the thing, he added, " You had no need to send for
painters elsewhere when you had a master in your
own house; but perhaps he did not know then how
to mix his colours. But now that he knows and can
do it all, I am no longer any good, and, recognizing
his talents, I am content to take nothing for my
work, but leave to return to Florence."

The bishop hearing the story, though it displeased

him, could not restrain his laughter, particularly considering that an animal should have played a joke upon the greatest joker in the world. So when they had talked and laughed the matter over, Buonamico set to work a third time and finished the picture. And the monkey as a punishment was shut up in a great wooden cage and kept where Buonamico worked until he had quite finished, and no one can imagine the grimaces and gesticulations that the little animal made with his face and his hands and his whole body at seeing some one else work and not being able to help.

The work in the chapel being finished, the bishop, either in jest or from some caprice, ordered that Buffalmacco should paint on the façade of his palace an eagle on the back of a lion which it had killed. [1] The crafty painter having promised to do what the bishop wished, had a great screen erected, saying he did not wish to be seen painting such a subject. And there, shut in all by himself, he painted the contrary of what the bishop desired, a lion tearing an eagle. When he had finished, he asked leave of the bishop to go to Florence for some colours that he needed. And having locked up his screen, he went to Florence, intending to return no more to the bishop, who seeing the time going on and the painter not returning, had the screen opened, and

[1] The eagle being the emblem of Arezzo and the lion of Florence.

found that the painter had been sharper than he. Then, moved to great anger, he published his ban against him, which Buonamico hearing, he sent to bid him do his worst. But finally the bishop, considering that it was he who had begun the joke, and that it served him right to have it turned against him, pardoned Buonamico, and rewarded him liberally for his labours. And more than that, not long after he fetched him again to Arezzo, and gave him many things to do in the old cathedral, treating him as his familiar and most faithful servant. But lest I should be too long if I were to tell of all the jokes that Buonamico Buffalmacco played, as well as of all the pictures that he painted, I will end by saying that he died at the age of seventy-eight, and was nursed in his illness by the Society of the Misericordia, for he was very poor, and had spent more than he earned, being a man of that nature.

CHAPTER III.

ANDREA DI CIONE ORCAGNA, SPINELLO, DELLO,
AND PAOLO UCCELLO.

IT is rarely the case that a man is excellent in one thing who could not easily learn another; and so we find that Orcagna the Florentine was painter, sculptor, architect, and poet. Born in Florence, he began as a boy the study of sculpture under Andrea Pisano; then he gave himself up to the study of drawing, and aided by Nature, who desired to make him a universal genius, he practised colouring in distemper and fresco, and succeeded so well with the aid of Bernardo, his brother, that this Bernardo took him with him to paint in S. Maria Novella, and by the works he painted in company with his brother, his fame spread so far that he was summoned to Pisa to paint in the Campo Santo.

Afterwards he gave himself with all his might to the study of architecture, thinking it might be of use to him. Nor did he mistake, for in the year 1355

the commune of Florence, having bought some
houses near the palace that they might enlarge the
Piazza, and make a place where the citizens might
retire under cover in winter and in time of rain,
ordered designs to be made for a magnificent loggia
near the palace. Among the designs made by the
best masters in the city Orcagna's was universally
approved and accepted as the best, the most beautiful, and most magnificent. So he began the work,
and brought it to a conclusion in a little time.

And a little after the company of Orsanmichele,
having in their possession much money, chiefly from
the alms presented to the Madonna there during the
mortality of 1348, resolved to make over her a chapel,
or rather a tabernacle, not only carved in marble
and adorned with precious stones, but also with
mosaics and bronze-work, so that it should surpass
in material and in excellent work everything made
before that time. And the charge being given to
Orcagna, he made many designs for it, until one
pleased the governors as better than all the others,
and the whole matter was left to his judgment.
And he giving to different masters from many
countries the other parts, kept for himself and his
brother all the figures in the work; and when it was
finished he caused it to be built up and joined
together without cement with fastenings of copper
and lead, that the polished marble might not be
stained, which succeeded so well that the whole

chapel seems to be cut out of one piece of marble.
But what great efforts he made in that dark age to
display his subtle genius is chiefly seen in a great
work in relief of the Twelve Apostles watching the
Madonna borne up to heaven by angels. For one of
the apostles he sculptured himself as he was, aged,
with shaven face, with his cowl about his head.
Below he wrote upon the marble these words,
"Andreas Cionis pictor Florentinus Oratorii archima-
gister extitit hujus, MCCCLIX." The building of
the loggia and the tabernacle cost ninety-six thousand gold florins, which were very well spent, for
whether as regards architecture, sculpture, or ornament, it is as beautiful as anything of those times,
and such that it will always keep alive the name of
Andrea Orcagna, who used on his paintings to
write, "Fece Andrea di Cione scultore," and on his
sculpture, "Fece Andrea di Cione pittore."

In the year 1350 was formed the Company and
Fraternity of the Painters in Florence, for the masters
were there in great numbers, and considered that the
arts of design had been born again in Tuscany, and
indeed in Florence itself. They put their company
under the protection of S. Luke the Evangelist, and
their oratory was the larger chapel of S. Maria
Nuova. The company was ruled by two councillors
and two treasurers, and when it was formed, Jacopo
di Casentino painted the picture for their chapel
representing S. Luke pourtraying the Virgin.

This Jacopo di Casentino had for his pupil the painter Spinello. For Luca Spinelli having gone to dwell at Arezzo at a time when the Ghibellines were driven out of Florence, there was born to him there a son to whom he gave the name of Spinello. He was so naturally inclined to painting that when he was a mere boy, and almost without teaching, he seemed to know much that those who have been under the discipline of the best masters do not know. Having formed a friendship with Jacopo di Casentino while he was working in Arezzo, he learnt somewhat from him, but before he was twenty years old he became a far greater master than old Jacopo was.

Beginning soon then to acquire a name as a good painter, Spinello was called to Florence, and painted in the churches of S. Niccolò and S. Maria Maggiore, and in other places, until the sixty citizens who governed Arezzo recalled him, and gave him work in the old cathedral outside the city.

A little before this time a number of good and honourable citizens had begun to go round collecting alms for the poor to aid them in their need; and in the plague of the year 1348, the good men of this fraternity, called the Fraternity of S. Mary of Mercy, acquired so great a name by helping the poor and sick, burying the dead and like works of charity, that gifts and legacies fell into their hands until they became possessors of the third part of the wealth of Arezzo. Spinello therefore, being of the fraternity, and having often to visit the sick and bury the dead, painted for the company in the church of S. Laurentino and Bergentino, a Madonna spreading her mantle over the people of Arezzo, among whom are many of the first men of the fraternity, painted from life, with the wallet on their shoulder, and the wooden mallet in their hands that they used in knocking at the doors when they went seeking alms.

In the church of S. Stefano he painted a Madonna giving the Child a rose, which was held in such veneration by the people of Arezzo that when the church was pulled down, regardless of difficulty and expense, they cut it out of the wall and carried it into the city and placed it in a chapel, that they might honour it with the same devotion as heretofore. Nor was this strange, for Spinello had a natural power of giving to his figures a certain simple grace, so that his saints, and especially his virgins, breathe a divine holiness, which draws men to hold them in the highest reverence. Having painted in many other cities whither his fame carried him, he returned to Arezzo, his home, or rather that which he considered his home, at the age of seventy-seven, and was received by his friends and relatives with affection, and held in honour to the end of his life, which was in the ninety-second year of his age. And although he was very old when he returned, and being rich, might have ceased from working, he knew not how to rest, but took upon him to paint for the

4

Company of S. Agnolo the story of S. Michael. He painted the Fall of the Angels, who are changed into devils as they fall from heaven, and St. Michael in the air fighting with the old serpent with seven heads and ten horns, and Lucifer changed already into a horrible beast. And because Spinello took great pleasure in making him horrible and deformed, it is said that the figure as he had painted it appeared to him in a dream, demanding why he had made him so ugly and done him so much injury with his pencil. He then awaking from his sleep, could not cry out from the greatness of his terror, but such a trembling fell upon him that his wife awoke and hastened to his succour. He was near dying of terror at the moment, and though he lingered a short time with an affrighted air and wide staring eyes, yet it led to his death. Such a sad event grieved the Aretines much, and they lamented him for his talents and goodness, although he was so old. He died at the age of ninety, and was buried in S. Agostino, where may be seen a stone bearing his arms, designed by himself, containing a hedgehog.

Although Dello the Florentine has a name as a painter only, his first works were in sculpture. But not only was he changeable by nature, he also perceived that he earned little, and that his poverty required him to change. So he applied himself to painting and succeeded, especially in little figures. At that time it was the custom of the people to have in their chambers great wooden chests of various forms, and every one used to have them painted with stories from the myths of Ovid and other poets, or hunting scenes, or jousts, or tales of love, according to the taste of each one. And in the same way were painted the beds and chairs and other furniture of the rooms. This practice was long in fashion, and the most excellent painters employed themselves in such work with no such sense of shame as many would feel now in painting and gilding such things. Dello then, being a good painter and well skilled especially, as we have said, in little pictures, spent many years in painting chests and chairs and such things, and particularly he painted for Giovanni di Medici the whole furniture of a room, which was considered marvellous and most beautiful of its kind. It is said that Donatello, then a youth, aided him, making with stucco, gesso, and paste ornaments in bas-relief, which being gilded brought out well the painted pictures. Afterwards Dello went to Spain into the king's service, where he obtained such favour that no artist could desire more. And though it is not known what works he did in those parts, yet as he returned very rich and with great honour, we may suppose that they were many and fine and good. But after having been royally rewarded for his labours for some years, the desire arose within him to return to Florence, that he might show his friends how from extreme poverty he had risen to

great riches. He asked therefore leave of the king,
and he not only granted it graciously, although he
would willingly have retained him, but in gratitude
for his service this most generous king made him
a knight. So he returned to Florence and demanded
his pension and the confirmation of his privileges,
but they were refused him by Filippo Spano degli
Scolari, who had just returned victorious over the
Turks, as grand seneschal of the king of Hungary.
Dello thereupon wrote in haste to the king com-
plaining of the injury done him; and the king inter-
ceded for him with the Signory so warmly that the
desired honour was granted him. It is said that
Dello, returning to his house on horseback with his
banner, and clad in brocade, as he passed along the
Vacchereccia, where were then many goldsmiths'
shops, was jeered at by certain who had known him
familiarly in youth, and he turning to the side where
he heard the voices, made a gesture of contempt,
and without saying anything passed on his way, so
that none perceived it but those who had scoffed at
him. But seeing by this and other signs that the
envy felt towards him was as great as the unkindness
shown him when he was poor, he determined to
return to Spain. There he was received with great
favour and looked upon kindly, and there he lived
and laboured like a lord, painting always attired in
a brocaded apron. Thus retiring before envy, he
dwelt in honour with the king. He died at the age

of forty-nine, and was buried honourably. He was
not a very good draughtsman, but was one of the
first to show good judgment in the marking of the
muscles in the human body. His portrait was
painted by Paolo Uccello in S. Maria Novella, in the
picture representing the drunkenness of Noah.

Paolo Uccello would have been the cleverest and
most original genius since the time of Giotto if he
would have studied figures and animals as much as
he studied and wasted his time over perspective,
for although it is an ingenious and fine science, yet
he who pursues it out of measure throws away his
time, makes his manner dry, and often himself
becomes solitary and strange, melancholy and poor,
as Paolo Uccello did. Donatello, his great friend,
many times said to him when Paolo showed him his
circles and his squares and his balls with seventy-
two faces, all drawn in perspective, and all the other
fancies in which he wasted his time, "Eh, Paolo,
this perspective of yours makes you leave what is
certain for the uncertain; these are things which
are no use except for men who make inlaid work."
In S. Miniato, outside Florence, he painted the lives
of the Fathers, in which pictures he made the fields
azure, the cities red, and the buildings varied, according to his own pleasure; and in this he did wrong,
for things that we suppose to be of stone ought not
to be painted of any other colour. It is said that
while Paolo was engaged on this work, the abbot

of the place gave him scarcely anything but cheese
to eat; and this thing becoming an annoyance,
Paolo, who was timid, determined not to go there
any more to work.   And when the abbot sent for him,
and he heard himself asked for by the friars, he
always sent word that he was not at home; and if
by chance he met a couple of that order in Florence
he would set off running as hard as he could to
escape them.   But one day two of the youngest and
more curious of them overtook him and asked him
why he did not come to finish the work he had
begun, and why he took to flight whenever he met
any of the friars.   Paolo replied, " You have ruined
me altogether, so that not only do I flee from you,
but I dare not pass by any place where there are
carpenters; for your abbot, with his tarts and soup
all made of cheese, has so filled me with it that I am
afraid of being boiled down for glue, and if I had
gone on any longer I should have left off being
Paolo and become cheese."   The friars returned
home in fits of laughter and told the abbot about it;
whereupon he persuaded him to return to his work,
promising that other food besides cheese should be
supplied him.

He painted many pictures of animals, of which he
was very fond.   He made a great study of them and
had always in his house paintings of birds, cats, and
dogs, and any kind of strange animal that he could
get a drawing of, not being able to keep live animals

because he was poor; and because he delighted most
in birds (*uccelli*) he was surnamed Paolo Uccello.
Among other pictures of animals he made some
lions fighting together, which by their motions and
terrible fierceness seem to be alive. But the most
strange was a serpent fighting with a lion, exhibiting
his fury in fierce contortions, with the poison issuing
from his eyes and mouth, while a peasant woman
who is present taking care of an ox, most beautifully
foreshortened, is running away in terror.

In the cloister of S. Maria Novella also he painted
the creation of the animals and the deluge. He was
the first who gained a name for landscapes, carrying
them to more perfection than any other painter
before him. In S. Maria del Fiore he also made a
monument to Sir John Hawkwood, the English
captain of the Florentines, who died in the year
1393, a horse of extraordinary size, with the captain
upon it. The work was considered and really is
very fine for pictures of that sort, and if Paolo had
not made the horse moving his legs on one side
only, which horses do not naturally do or they
would fall, the work would be perfect. Perhaps
he made the mistake because he was not used to
ride or to study horses as he did other animals;
but the foreshortening of the horse is very fine.
Paolo was taken by Donatello to Padua where he
was working, and there he painted some giants,
which were so fine that Andrea Mantegna held

them in the highest esteem. He also painted in
fresco the loggia of the Peruzzi, introducing in the
corners the four elements accompanied by an appropriate animal; for the earth there was a mole, for
water a fish, for fire a salamander, and for air the
chameleon, which lives upon it and takes every
colour. And because he had never seen a chameleon,
in his great simplicity he made in its stead a camel
opening its mouth and swallowing the air to fill its
stomach.

Such great pains did Paolo take in his works that
he left behind him chests full of drawings, as I have
heard from his relatives themselves. In his house
he had a picture of five men who had distinguished
themselves in art: Giotto the painter, as the beginning and light of art, Filippo di Ser Brunellesco
for architecture, Donatello for sculpture, himself
for perspective and animals, and for mathematics
Giovanni Manetti, his friend.

It is said that being entrusted with the painting
of S. Thomas over the gate of the church dedicated
to that saint in the Old Market, he resolved to put
into the work all he knew, and to show how much
he was capable of; and so he made a screen round
him that none might be able to see his work until it
was finished. And one day Donatello, meeting him
all alone asked him, "What is this work of yours
which you keep shut up so close?" To which Paolo
replied, "You will see in time." Donatello would

not urge him any more, expecting to see something marvellous. But one morning, going into the old market to buy fruit, he saw Paolo uncovering his work, and saluting him courteously, Paolo called upon him to say what he thought of his picture, eagerly desiring to know his opinion. Donatello looking at the work carefully, replied, " Eh, Paolo, now that it is time to cover it up you are uncovering it." Upon this Paolo was greatly afflicted, seeing that by this his last effort he had earned much more blame than he hoped to have earned praise ; and, as if he had disgraced himself, not having courage to walk abroad any longer, he shut himself up in his house, giving himself up to perspective, and remained poor and obscure until his death. His wife used to say that Paolo would sit studying perspective all night, and when she called him to come to bed he would answer, "Oh, what a sweet thing this perspective is ! " And if it was sweet to him, his work has made it valuable and useful indeed to those who have studied it after him.

CHAPTER IV.

LUCA DELLA ROBBIA was born in Florence, and was put by his father to learn the goldsmith's trade. But having made trial of his skill in some things in marble and bronze, he gave himself up entirely to sculpture, carving by day and drawing by night, with such earnestness that many times when his feet were chilled with the cold at night, rather than give up his drawing, he would put them into a basket of shavings to warm them. He was scarcely fifteen years of age when he was taken to Rimini to work with other sculptors on the monument which Sigismondo di Pandolfo Malatesti was raising to his wife. He was called back, however, to work on the campanile of S. Maria del Fiore, and was afterwards, at the request of Vieri de' Medici, a very popular citizen who loved him much, entrusted with the marble ornaments of the organ. In this work he represented the choristers singing, and although it was sixteen braccia from the ground, he worked it with great care. Donatello, however, who made the ornaments of the organ opposite, worked with more judgment and experience, making it rougher and less finished, so that it appeared better at a distance than Luca's.

But after he had finished these and other works for the cathedral, reckoning up how much he had received and the time he had spent upon it, and seeing that the profit was very little and the fatigue very great, he resolved to let marble and bronze alone and see if he could not earn more in some other way. And considering that working in clay was easy, he set himself to find a way by which it might be defended from the injuries of time. And after many experiments he found a way of covering it with a glaze by which it was made almost eternal. And not being satisfied at having made an invention so useful, especially for damp places, he added a method by which he could give it colour, to the marvel and great pleasure of every one. The fame of these works soon spread not only through Italy, but through all Europe, and the demand was so great that the Florentine merchants kept him continually at work and sent them all over the world. Not being able to supply them as fast as they required, he took his brothers away from the chisel and set them to the work, and they made much more by it than they had ever done before. If he had lived longer, no doubt greater works would have issued from his hands, but death, which carries off the best, took him away.

After his death there were left his brothers, Ottaviano and Agostino, and of the same family was Andrea, who died in 1528. I remember talking to him when I was a boy and hearing him say he had helped to carry Donatello to the grave, and I remember the good old man seemed to take much pride in the recollection. Andrea left two sons, Luca and Girolamo, who devoted themselves to sculpture. Of these two Luca specially applied himself to the gla: :d works. But when they died not only was their family extinct, but the art also was lost, for although some have taken up that kind of sculpture, none have ever arrived at the excellence of old Luca or Andrea or any others of that family.

There is no doubt that those in every city who by their merits obtain fame become a blessed light to those who are born after them. For there is nothing that arouses the minds of men, and makes them indifferent to the hardships of study, so much as the honour and advantage that the labour may bring them. This Lorenzo di Cione Ghiberti, otherwise Di Bartoluccio, knew well. He in his first years was put to the art of the goldsmith, but delighting more in the arts of sculpture and design, he studied colours and also cast little figures in bronze. About this time the Signory of Florence with the Guild of the Merchants, seeing that there were at that time many excellent sculptors, both Florentines and strangers, determined that they would make the second pair of gates for

... there were but his brothers,
... . of the same family was
... 1518. I remember talking to
... a boy and hearing him say he had
... . to the grave, and I re-
... . seemed to take much pride
... . left two sons, Luca and
... . themselves to sculpture. Of
... . applied himself to the
... . when they died not only was
... . but one art also was lost, for
... . them to say that kind of sculpture,
... . the excellence of old Luca
or .... that family.

The ...... at those in every city who by
...... its .... become a blessed light to
.... after them. But there is nothing
.... minds of men, and makes them ...
.... of study, so much as the
.... that the labour ...... them.
...... Ghiberti, ...
...... held these was was put to
.... but Ghiberti made in the
.... studied ...... and
.... in bronze. About this time the
.... with the Guild of the Merchants,
.... were at that time many excellent
...... Florentines ...... and ...... remained
...... would make the second pair of gates for

SINGING BOYS. By LUCA DELLA ROBBIA.

S. Giovanni, the oldest and chief church of that city.
So they made known to all the best masters in Italy
that they should come to Florence and make trial
of their skill, producing a subject picture worked in
bronze, like one of those which Andrea Pisano
had made in the first gate. Bartoluccio Ghiberti
thereupon wrote to Lorenzo his son,[1] who was
working in Pesaro, urging him to return to Florence,
for this was an opportunity of making himself
known and showing his skill. These words so moved
Lorenzo that although Pandolfo Malatesti and all
his court were heaping him with caresses, and
would scarcely let him go, he took his leave of
them, and neither promise nor reward would detain
him, for it seemed to him to be a thousand years
before he could get to Florence. So setting forth
he came prosperously to his own city. Many
strangers had already arrived and made known their
coming to the consuls of the guild. They made
choice of seven, three being Florentines and the rest
Tuscans, ordaining for them a certain provision of
money, and requiring that within a year each one
should finish one subject in bronze of the same size
as those of the first gate. And the subject was
Abraham sacrificing Isaac his son, for they thought
that it contained all the difficulties of the art, landscape, figures nude and draped, and animals. Those
who took part in the contest were Filippo di Ser

[1] Or rather stepson.

Brunellesco, Donatello,[1] and Lorenzo, all Florentines; and Jacopo della Quercia of Sienna and Niccolò d'Arezzo his pupil, Francesco di Vandabrina, and Simone da Colle, famous for his bronzes, and they all made promise to finish the work in the time appointed. So each one set to work, and with all diligence and study put forth all his strength and knowledge to surpass the others in excellence, working secretly and keeping concealed what they did that they might not do the same things. Lorenzo alone, who worked by Bartoluccio's counsel, and who was required by him to make essays and many models before he resolved upon using them for the work, continually brought in the citizens to see, and sometimes strangers who were passing through, if they understood the matter, that he might hear their opinions; and so it came about that the model was very well done and without any defect. And having made the mould and cast it in bronze, it came out very well indeed, and he, with Bartoluccio his father, polished it with such patience and earnestness that it could not have been finished better.

So the time being come when they were to be exhibited in competition, they were all finished and brought before the Guild of the Merchants for judgment. And when the consuls and many other citizens had seen them, opinions were very diverse about them. And there came many strangers to

[1] This is a mistake.

Florence, painters and sculptors and some goldsmiths, called by the consuls to aid them to give
judgment, with others of that trade who dwelt at
Florence. The number of them was thirty-four,
each one most skilful in his art. And although their
opinions were different, one being pleased with the
manner of this one, and another with that, nevertheless they agreed that Filippo Brunellesco and
Lorenzo had composed and finished the subject better
than Donatello, although there was good drawing
in his. Jacopo della Quercia had good figures, but
there was no finish, although it was done with
diligence. Francesco di Vandabrina's work had good
heads and was well polished, but was confused in the
composition. That by Simone da Colle was a good
cast, that being his special art, but the design was
not good. Niccolò d'Arezzo's figures were stunted
and the work was not well polished. Only the piece
which Lorenzo had brought as his specimen, which
may still be seen in the merchants' hall, was perfect
in all its parts; the work was well designed and well
composed, the figures were graceful and their attitudes
very beautiful, and it was finished with so much care
that it had no appearance of having been cast and
worked upon with iron tools, but seemed rather
to have been breathed into existence.

Then Donatello and Filippo, seeing the care that
Lorenzo had taken with his work, withdrew into a
corner, and talking together resolved that the work

ought to be entrusted to Lorenzo, for it seemed to them that it would be both for public and private good that Lorenzo being young, for he was no more than twenty, would by the practice be enabled to bring forth those greater fruits of which this was a promise; and in their judgment he had executed it more excellently than the others, so that it would be rather the part of envy to take the work from him than a virtue to give it up to him.

Therefore the work being entrusted to Lorenzo, he made a wooden frame of the proper size, and worked all the ornaments and decorations of the gate, and those that were to surround each compartment, and having dried the model in a house which he had bought over against S. Maria Nuova, where now stands the weavers' hospital, he made a great furnace, which I can remember to have seen, and cast the frame in metal. But as fortune would have it, it did not come well, so without losing courage, or being dismayed, he made another mould so quickly that none knew of it, and cast it again, and this time it came out excellently well. And so continuing his work he cast each subject by itself, and fitted it into its place. And the work was brought to perfection without sparing time or fatigue, and the composition of each work was so well arranged that it deserves that praise, and greater, which Filippo had given to the first part. And so he was honoured by his fellow citizens and greatly praised by the artists both of his own land and strangers. The work with the ornaments round, of animals and festoons of fruit, cost twenty-two thousand florins, and the gates weighed thirty-four thousand pounds.

After this the fame of Lorenzo went on increasing every day, and he worked for an infinite number of persons, making for Pope Martin a clasp for his cope, with figures in high relief, and a mitre with leaves of gold, and among them many little figures which were held to be most beautiful. Also when Pope Eugenius came to Florence, to the council held in 1439, and saw the works of Lorenzo, he caused him to make for him a mitre of gold, in weight fifteen pounds, and the pearls of it weighed five and a half pounds.

And when Florence saw that the works of their great artist were so much praised, it was determined by the merchants to entrust to him the third pair of gates of S. Giovanni. And although the one he had made before had been by their orders made with ornaments like those on the gates of Andrea Pisano, yet seeing that Lorenzo had surpassed his, they gave him leave to make it in any manner he liked, so that it should be the most highly adorned, the richest, most perfect, and most beautiful that could be imagined. Neither was he to regard time or expense, but as he had surpassed all other sculptors, so was he to surpass all his other works.

5

Lorenzo therefore began his work, and put into it all that he knew. And in truth it may be said that the work is perfect in everything, and is the most beautiful work in the world that has ever been seen in ancient or modern times. And Lorenzo ought to be praised in truth, for one day Michael Angelo Buonarroti stopping to look at the work, some one asked him what he thought of it, and if these gates were beautiful, and he answered, "They are so beautiful that they might well be the gates of paradise." Praise truly just, and given by one who could judge!

Lorenzo was aided in polishing and finishing the work after it was cast by many young men who afterwards became excellent masters, as Filippo Brunellesco, Paolo Uccello, Antonio del Pollaiuolo, and others. And besides the payment which the consuls of the guild gave him, the Signory bestowed upon him a good estate near the abbey of Settimo. Nor was it long before he was received among the Signory, and honoured with the supreme magistracy of the city. For which the Florentines deserve to be praised for their grateful spirit, as they have deserved to be blamed for the little gratitude they have shown towards others.

CHAPTER V.

FILIPPO DI SER BRUNELLESCO.

IT is a habit of Nature when she makes one man very great in any profession, not to make him alone, but at the same time and in the same place to produce another to rival him, that they may aid each other by emulation. And that this is true may be seen by the example of Florence, which produced at one epoch Filippo, Donatello, Lorenzo, Paolo Uccello, and Masaccio, each one most excellent in his way. This last, who came from Castello San Giovanni di Valdarno was a most absent-minded man, and seemed like one who having fixed his mind on things of art only, cared little for himself and less for others. And because he would never trouble himself about the things of the world, not even about dressing himself, and never took the pains to get money from those who owed it him, unless he were in extreme need, he was by every one nicknamed Masaccio [1] for Tommaso, which was his real name, and this not because he was a bad man, but merely from his slovenliness, for he was goodness itself, and as ready

[1] Big Tom, a contemptuous epithet.

to do another a service as any one could desire. All the most celebrated sculptors and painters from his time until now have studied his works in the Brancacci chapel, as Lionardo da Vinci, Perugino, the divine Michael Angelo, Raffaello da Urbino, Andrea del Sarto, and many more, and if I have not mentioned many Florentines and strangers who have gone to that chapel to study there, it is because where the heads of the art go, there the members are sure to follow. Yet although his works have always been held in such reputation, it is the firm belief of many that he would have brought forth much greater fruit if death had not carried him off, at the age of twenty-six, so suddenly that there were not wanting those who laid it down to poison. It is said that when Filippo di Ser Brunellesco heard of his death, he said, "We have suffered a great loss in Masaccio," and mourned for him deeply.

There are some whom Nature has created little of stature but with a soul of greatness and a heart of such immeasurable daring that if they do not set themselves to difficult and almost impossible things, and do not complete them to the wonder of those who behold, they have no peace in their lives. Thus it was with Filippo di Ser Brunellesco, who was small in stature like Giotto, but great in genius. His father, Ser Brunellesco, taught him in his childhood the first principles of letters, in which he showed himself intelligent but careless of perfecting himself in these matters. Therefore, seeing him occupied with matters of art, he put him under a goldsmith, to Filippo's great satisfaction. Having become skilled in setting stones, and in niello work, and in the science of the motion of weights and wheels, not content with this, there awoke within him a great desire for the study of sculpture. And Donatello, then a young man, being held in esteem as a sculptor, Filippo began to hold intercourse with him, and such an affection sprang up between them that it seemed as if the one could not live without the other. Filippo, who was capable of many things, was held also by those who understood such matters to be a good architect. He studied also perspective, and taught it to Masaccio his friend.

Messer Paolo dal Pozzo Toscanelli, having returned from his studies, invited Filippo with other friends to supper in a garden, and the discourse falling on mathematical subjects, Filippo formed a friendship with him and learned geometry from him. And although he was not learned, he would reason on all matters from his own practical experience so as frequently to confound Toscanelli. He also applied himself to the study of the sacred scriptures, never failing to be present at the disputations or lectures of learned men, and making such good use of his wonderful memory that Messer Paolo used to say when he heard Filippo argue, he seemed to him a new St. Paul.

Filippo, as we have said, entered into competition with Lorenzo and the others for the gates of S. Giovanni, but when the work was assigned to Lorenzo at the request of Filippo and Donatello, they determined to set out together from Florence and to spend some years in Rome that Filippo might study architecture and Donatello sculpture. And when he came to Rome and saw the grandeur of the buildings and the perfection of the form of the temples, he remained lost in thought and like one out of his mind, and he and Donatello set themselves to measure them and to draw out the plan of them, sparing neither time nor expense. And Filippo gave himself up to the study of them, so that he cared neither to eat or to sleep, having two great ideas in his mind, the one to restore the knowledge of good architecture, hoping to leave behind no less a memory of himself than Cimabue and Giotto had done, and the other to find a way, if it were possible, of raising the cupola of S. Maria del Fiore in Florence, the difficulty of which was so great that since the death of Arnolfo Lapi none had had courage enough to attempt it. He confided his intention neither to Donatello or any soul living, but gave himself no rest until he had considered all the difficulties of the Pantheon and had noted and drawn all the ancient vaulted roofs, continually studying this matter, and if by chance they found any pieces of capitals or columns they set to work and had them dug out.

And the story ran through Rome that they were "treasure seekers," the people thinking that they studied divination to find treasures, it having befallen them once to find an ancient pitcher filled with medals.

Then money becoming scarce with Filippo, he set himself to work for the goldsmiths, and remained thus alone in Rome when Donatello returned to Florence. Neither did he cease from his studies until he had drawn every kind of building, temples round and square and eight-sided, basilicas, aqueducts, baths, arches, and others, and the different orders, Doric, Ionic, and Corinthian, until he was able to see in imagination Rome as she was before she fell into ruins.

In the year 1407 he returned to Florence, and the same year there was held a meeting of architects and engineers to consider how to raise the cupola of S. Maria del Fiore. Among them came Filippo, and gave it as his opinion that it should not be done according to the design of Arnolfo, but in another fashion, of which he made a model.

Some months after, Filippo being one morning in the Piazza of S. Maria del Fiore with Donatello and other artists, talking about ancient sculpture, Donatello began telling them how when he was returning from Rome he had journeyed by Orvieto to see the famous marble façade of the cathedral, and afterwards passing through Cortona went into the church there and found a most beautiful piece of ancient sculpture, which was then a rare thing, for they had not then disinterred such an abundance as they have in our times. So Donatello, going on to describe the manner of the work and its perfection and excellence, kindled such an ardent desire in Filippo to see it that without saying where he was going, he set out on foot in his mantle and hood and sandals, and was carried to Cortona by the love he bore to art. The sculpture pleasing him much, he made a drawing of it with the pen, and returned to Florence before Donatello or any one else had discovered that he was gone. And when he showed him the careful drawing he had made, Donatello marvelled greatly seeing his love for art.

The other architects meanwhile being dismayed at the difficulties in raising the cupola, the masters of the works in S. Maria and the consuls of the Guild of the Woollen Merchants assembled together and sent to pray Filippo to come to them. And he being come they laid before him the difficulties little and great which the architects felt who were also present. And Filippo answered them, "Sirs, there is no doubt that in great undertakings you have always to encounter great difficulties, and in this one of yours there are greater than you perhaps imagine, for I do not think that even the ancients ever raised such a vaulted roof as this will be. And I, having considered it much, have never been able to come to

any conclusion, the width as well as the height of
the building dismaying me. But remembering that
it is a temple consecrated to God and the Virgin, I
believe that the wisdom and skill of any one who
undertook it would not be allowed to fail, and if it
were my affair I would resolutely set myself to find
out a way. But if you resolve upon doing it you
must take counsel not alone of me, who am not
sufficient to give counsel in so great a matter, but
summon to Florence upon a fixed day within a
year's time architects, not only Tuscan and Italian
but German and French, and those of every nation,
and lay before them this matter, that having been
discussed and decided by so many masters, it may be
entrusted to him who has the best judgment and
knows the best way."

And this counsel pleased them well, and they
desired that he also would consider the matter and
make a model for it. But he made believe not to
care about the matter, and took his leave of them
to return to Rome. And they seeing that their
prayers availed not to stop him, made many of his
friends implore him also, and when he would not be
moved, the members of the council voted him an
offering of money. But he, keeping firm to his
resolution, left Florence and returned to Rome,
where he applied himself to continual study of the
matter, thinking, as was true, that none but he could
accomplish it.

So the Florentine merchants who dwell in France and England and Spain were commanded to obtain from the princes of those lands, without sparing expense, the most skilled and gifted men in those regions. And when the year 1420 was come, there were assembled in Florence all these masters from other lands and those of Tuscany, and the skilled artificers of Florence itself, and Filippo returned from Rome. And they came together in S. Maria del Fiore, with the consuls and members of the guild, and some ingenious men chosen from among the citizens that the minds of all might be known, and the manner of raising the dome decided upon. So one by one each architect was called upon to give his opinion and describe the way in which it should be done. And it was a fine thing to hear the strange and diverse opinions in the matter. For some proposed that it should be built of sponge-stone that the weight might be less, and many agreed that it would be best to put a pillar in the middle, while there were not wanting those who suggested that they should fill the space with earth, mixing money with it, and when the dome was built give leave to every one to take the money, by which means the earth would be cleared away without expense. Filippo alone declared that he could make a vaulted roof without much wood, without pillars or supports, and with little expense of arches. It seemed to all who heard him that he had said something foolish, and they mocked him and laughed at him, saying he was speaking like a madman. Then Filippo, being offended, said, "Though you laugh at me, you shall know that it can be done in no other manner." And as he grew warm in explaining his ideas, they doubted him the more, and held him to be a chattering fool. And when they had bidden him depart several times and he would not go, he was carried out by force, all supposing him to be mad. And this was how it came about that Filippo used to say afterwards that he dared not at that time pass along any part of the city lest it should be said, "There goes that madman." So the consuls in the assembly were left altogether confused with the difficult methods proposed by the other masters, and Filippo's plan, which seemed to them foolish. And on his part Filippo was many times tempted to leave Florence, but desiring to conquer, he had to arm himself with patience. He might have shown a little model that he had made, but he would not, knowing how little the consuls understood the matter, and the jealousy of the artists, and the unstable character of the citizens, who favoured now one, now another. And I do not marvel at this, for in that city every one professes to know as much as skilled masters themselves, although there are few who really understand such things.

So Filippo, not having succeeded at the assembly, began to treat with them separately, talking now to

this consul, now to that member of the guild, and
to some of the citizens, showing them part of his
design.　And so having been stirred up by him,
they met again and disputed of the matter.　The
other architects desired that Filippo would tell all
his mind and show his model.　This he would not
do, but made a proposal that the building of the
cupola should be given to him who could make an
egg stand firmly on the smooth marble, for by doing
this he would show his skill.　And an egg being
brought, all the masters tried to make it stand upright, but none found the way.　And when they bade
Filippo set it up, he took it, and striking it on the
marble made it stand.　And the architects mur-
mured, saying that they could have done that; but
Filippo replied laughing that they could have built
the cupola, too, if they had seen his model and
designs.　So it was resolved that the charge of the
work should be entrusted to him.

But while he was making ready to begin to build,
there arose some who said that such a work as this
ought not to be entrusted to one only, as too great a
burden for one to bear alone.　And Lorenzo Ghiberti,
having obtained great credit by his gates of S.
Giovanni, and being beloved by certain who had
power with the government, he was joined with
Filippo in this work.　What was Filippo's bitter
despair when he heard of this may be imagined
from his desiring to leave Florence; and had it not

been for Donatello and Luca della Robbia, who comforted him, he would have gone out of his mind. He set to work with little will, knowing that he should have all the trouble and yet be obliged to share the honour and fame with Lorenzo. In this state of torment they went on working together until the end of 1426, when they had raised the walls twelve braccia, and it was time to begin works of wood and stone to strengthen it, which, being a difficult thing, he consulted Lorenzo to see whether he had considered this difficulty, and he was so barren of suggestions that he only replied that he would leave it to him. The answer pleased Filippo, for he thought he had found a way of driving him from the work. One morning, therefore, he did not come to the place, but took to his bed, and lay groaning and causing hot cloths to be brought him constantly, feigning himself sick.

So the masons, having waited for his orders in vain, went to Lorenzo, and asked what they were to do. But he replied that it was for Filippo to order, and they must wait for him. And one asked him, "Do you not know his mind?" and Lorenzo answered, "Yes, but I will do nothing without him." And this he said to excuse himself, for he had never seen Filippo's model. But when this had lasted two days the chief masons went to Filippo to ask what they were to do. And he answered, "You have Lorenzo, let him do a little." So there arose great murmuring among the men, some saying that Lorenzo was good at taking his salary, but at giving orders, no!

Then the wardens of S. Maria went to see Filippo, and after having condoled with him on his sickness, told him how it had brought all the building into confusion. But he answered with passionate words, "Is not he there—Lorenzo?" And they answered, "He will do nothing without you." "I could do very well without him," said Filippo.

But seeing that Lorenzo was willing to take his salary without any work for it, he thought of another way of bringing him to scorn; so, returning to his work, he made proposition to the wardens, Lorenzo being present, that as they had divided the salary so they should divide the work. "There are now two difficulties to be overcome, the one the matter of the scaffolding to bear the men, and the other the chain-work to bind the building together. Let Lorenzo take which he will, and I will do the other, that no time might be lost." Lorenzo, being forced in honour not to refuse, chose the chainwork, trusting in the advice of the masons, and remembering that there was something like it in S. Giovanni. So they set to work, and Filippo's scaffolds were made so that the men could work as if they were on firm ground. Lorenzo with great difficulty made the chainwork on one of the eight faces, and when it was finished the wardens took Filippo to see it, but he said nothing. But to his friends he said it ought to be secured in another way to that, and that it was not sufficient for the weight to be put upon it. And his words being heard, they called upon him to show how the thing ought to be done. So he brought out his models and designs, and they saw into what an error they had fallen in favouring Lorenzo. Then they made Filippo sole head and manager of the building, and commanded that none should work thereon but with his consent.

Lorenzo, although vanquished and shamed, was so favoured by his friends that he was allowed to go on drawing his salary, having proved that they could not legally withdraw it for three years.

So the works went forward, but the masons being urged on by Filippo more than they were used to, began to grow weary, and joining together in a body, they said it was hard work and perilous, and they would not go on without great pay, although they had more than was usual. Thereupon Filippo and those who had the management of the works, being displeased, took counsel together, and resolved on the Saturday evening to dismiss them all. And on the Monday following Filippo set ten Lombards to the work, and being constantly with them, saying, " Do this here, and do that there," he taught them in a day so much that for many weeks they were able to carry on the works. The masons, on the other hand, seeing themselves dismissed and their

work taken from them, and finding no other work
so profitable, sent men to intercede for them with
Filippo. But for many days he kept them in suspense,
and then received them at lower wages than they
had received before.

The building had now proceeded so far that it was
a long way for any one to climb, and much time was
lost in going down to dinner and to drink, for they
suffered much from thirst in the heat of the day. So
Filippo ordered that eating-houses should be opened
in the cupola, where wine should be | sold, and that
no one should leave his work till the evening, which
was a great convenience to them and profit to the
work.

Although he had now overcome envy and was
everywhere praised, he could not prevent all the
architects in Florence, after they had seen his model,
from producing others; even a lady of the Gaddi
family venturing to compete with him. He however
laughed at them all, and some of them having introduced in their models parts of Filippo's work, he
remarked one day when looking at them, " The next
model will be all mine." His own was infinitely
praised, but because people could not see the staircase leading up to the ball, they said it was defective.
So some of those presiding over the work came to
him concerning the matter, and Filippo, raising a
little piece of wood in his model, showed them the
staircase in one of the piers, formed like a pipe,

with bars of bronze on one side by which one could climb up. He did not live to see the lantern finished, but he left orders in his will that it should be done as it was in his model, otherwise he protested the building would fall.

While this work was going on, Filippo undertook many other buildings, and his fame was spread abroad, so that any one who desired to build sent for him, among whom were the Marquis of Mantua and Count Francesco Sforza. Cosimo de' Medici also proposing to build himself a palace, Filippo laid aside all his other occupations and made a large and most beautiful model for it. But Cosimo, thinking it too sumptuous a building, and fearing not so much the expense as the envy it would excite, did not have it put in execution. While he was working at the model, Filippo used to say he thanked fortune for the opportunity of designing a house, which he had desired for many years. Therefore when he heard that Cosimo had decided not to have it carried out, in his anger he broke it into a thousand pieces. But Cosimo afterwards repented not having followed Filippo's design.

Filippo was a facetious man in conversation, and would often give a witty answer. Lorenzo Ghiberti had bought a farm at Mount Morello, called Lepriano, on which he had to spend twice as much as it brought him in, so that it being an annoyance to him he sold it. Some one therefore asking Filippo what

6

was the best thing Lorenzo had ever done, expecting as they were enemies he would begin to find fault with his works, he answered, " Selling Lepriano." Filippo at his death was greatly lamented by other artists, especially by those who were poor, whom he often assisted. So having lived as a Christian should, he left behind him a fragrant memory of his goodness and his great talents.

CHAPTER VI.

DONATELLO.

FILIPPO'S friend Donato, who was always called Donatello, was born in Florence in the year 1383, and made many sculptures in his youth; but the first thing that caused him to be known was an Annunciation carved in stone for the church of S. Croce in Florence. For the same church he made a crucifix of wood, which he carved with extraordinary patience, and when it was done, thinking it a very fine piece of work, he showed it to Filippo that he might have his opinion upon it. Filippo, who expected from what Donatello had said to see something better, when he looked at it could not help smiling a little. Donatello, seeing it, prayed him as they were friends to speak his mind truly, upon which Filippo, who was frank enough, replied that he seemed to him to have put on the cross a peasant and not Jesus Christ, who was the man most perfect in everything that ever was born. Donatello, feeling the reproach more bitterly because he had expected praise, replied, "If it were as easy

to do a thing as to judge it, my Christ would not
look like a peasant, but take some wood yourself and
make one." Filippo without another word returned
home, and, saying nothing to any one, set to work
upon a crucifix, and aiming to surpass Donatello that
he might not condemn himself, he brought it to great
perfection after many months. Then one morning
he invited Donatello to dine with him. Donatello
accepted his invitation, and they went together to
Filippo's house. Coming to the old market, Filippo
bought some things and gave them to Donatello,
saying, "Go on to the house and wait for me, I am
just coming." So Donatello, going into the house,
found Filippo's crucifix arranged in a good light; and
stopping to consider it, he found it so perfect that,
overcome with surprise and admiration, he let his
apron drop, and the eggs and cheese and all the other
things that he was carrying in it fell to the ground
and were broken. Filippo, coming in and finding him
standing thus lost in astonishment, said, laughingly,
"What do you mean, Donatello? How are we to
dine when you have dropped all the things?" "I,"
said Donatello, "have had enough. If you want
anything, take it. To you it is given to do Christs,
and to me peasants."

Afterwards he made for the façade of S. Maria del
Fiore a Daniel and a S. John the Evangelist, and
within the same church, for the organ gallery, those
figures which, though they are only roughly sketched,

seem when you look at them to be alive and move.
For Donatello made his figures in such a way that in
the room where he worked they did not look half
as well as when they were put in their places. It
was so with the S. Mark, which in company with
Filippo he undertook for the joiners (though with
Filippo's goodwill he completed it all himself),
When the masters of the company saw ·it while
it was on the ground they did not recognize its
value, and stopped the work; but Donatello begged
them to let him put it up and work upon it, and
he would turn it into quite another figure. Then,
having set it up and screened it from view for a fortnight, when he uncovered it, although he had not
touched it, every one was astonished at it. For the
armourers he made a S. George armed, very full of
life, with all the beauty of youth and the courage
of the soldier.

For the façade of S. Maria del Fiore he made also
four figures, two of which were portraits from life,
one young Francesco Soderini, and the other
Giovanni de Barduccio Cherichini, which is now
called the *Zuccone*, the bald man. This being considered more beautiful than anything he had ever
done, Donatello used to swear by it, saying, "By
the faith I bear to my bald man." While he was
working upon it he would look at it and say,
"Speak, speak!"

Duke Cosimo de' Medici admired his talents so

much that he made him work for him constantly;
and he on his part bore such love to Cosimo that he
undertook what he wished at the least sign, and
obeyed him.   There is a story told of a Genoese
merchant who, by the mediation of Cosimo, prevailed upon Donatello to make a bronze head for him.
When it was finished, the merchant coming to pay
him, thought that Donatello asked too much, so the
matter was referred to Cosimo.   He had it brought
to the upper court of the palace and placed on the
wall overlooking the street, that it might be seen
better.   But when he tried to settle the difference,
he found the merchant's offer very much below
Donatello's demand, and turning to him he said it
was too little.   The merchant, who thought it too
much, answered that Donatello had worked upon it
for a month, or a little more, and that would give him
more than half a florin a day.   Donatello upon that
turned upon him in anger, thinking these words too
great an insult, and telling the merchant that he
had found means in a hundredth part of an hour to
destroy the work of a year, he gave the head a
sudden blow and knocked it down into the street,
where it was broken into many pieces, adding that it
was evident he was in the habit of bargaining about
beans and not statues.   The merchant repenting,
offered to give him double as much if he would
make it again, but neither his promises nor Cosimo's
entreaties could make him consent.

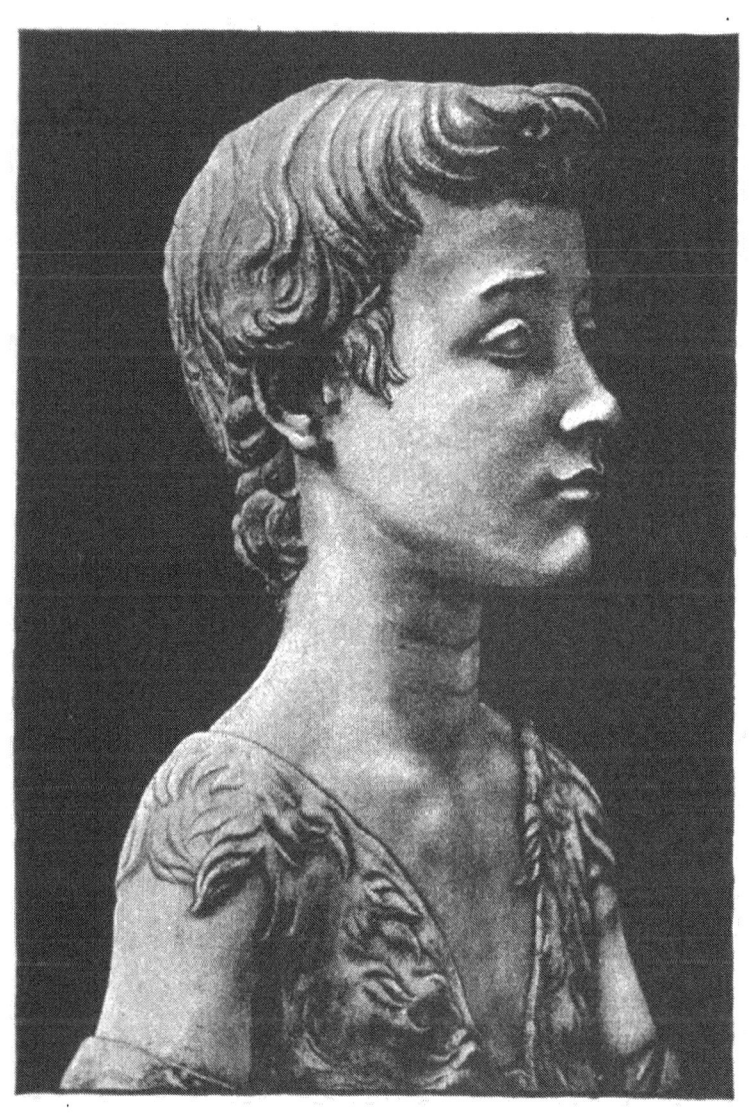

THE YOUNG ST. JOHN THE BAPTIST.   By DONATELLO.

In the houses of the Martelli are many works done by Donatello, and among them a David three braccia high, with many other things given to that family out of his love and devotion, particularly a S. John in high relief worked in marble, a most rare thing, belonging now to the heirs of Ruberto Martelli, who left command that it should never be pledged or sold or given away, under heavy penalties, in testimony of the kindness shown them by Donatello.

At this time the Signory of Venice, hearing the fame of him, sent for him to make the monument to Gattamelata in the city of Padua. He undertook it very gladly, and made the statue that stands in the Piazza of S. Antonio, with the horse chafing and neighing, and its proud, spirited rider. Donatello showed himself in this so admirable, both for proportion and execution, that truly it may be compared to any ancient work. The Paduans sought by every means to prevail upon him to become a citizen and to tarry there, giving him much work to do; but finding himself considered a marvel, and praised on all sides, he determined to return to Florence, saying if he stayed there longer he should forget all he knew, being praised so much, and that he must return to his own city to be continually found fault with, for this fault-finding would be the cause of his studying more, and therefore of greater glory.

To sum up, Donatello was so admirable in know-

ledge, in judgment, and in the practice of his art
that he may be said to have been the first to illus-
trate the art of sculpture among the moderns; and
he deserves the more commendation because in his
time few antiquities had been uncovered. He was
one of those who aroused in Cosimo de' Medici
the desire to bring antiquities into Florence. He
was most liberal and courteous, and kinder to his
friends than himself; nor did he care for money,
keeping it in a basket hanging from the ceiling,
where his workmen and friends could help themselves without saying anything to him. When he
got old, therefore, and could not work, he was supported by Cosimo and his friends. Cosimo dying,
recommended him to Piero his son, who, to carry
out his father's wishes, gave him a farm in Cafag-
giuolo on which he could live comfortably. Donatello
was greatly pleased, thinking he was now more than
secure from dying of hunger. But he had not held
it a year before he came to Piero and gave it him
back, saying that he could not give up all his quiet
to attend to domestic matters and to listen to the
troubles of the farmer, who was at him every third
day, now to complain that the wind had taken the
roof off the pigeon-house, now that all the cattle had
been taken to pay the taxes, and again that the
storm had destroyed his vines and fruit trees; that
he was weary of the trouble, and would rather die of
hunger than have to think of such things. Piero

laughed at his simplicity, and taking back the land, made him a provision of the same value in money paid him every week, with which he was quite content, and passed all the rest of his life as friend and servant of the Medici without trouble or care.

One of his pupils was Nanni d'Antonio di Banco, who, although he inherited riches and was not of low birth, yet delighting in sculpture, was not only not ashamed to learn it and to practise it, but obtained not a little glory in it. He was by nature rather slow, but modest, humble, and agreeable in conversation. The S. Philip in marble which is outside the Orsanmichele in Florence is from his hand. The work had been first allotted to Donatello by the guild of the shoemakers, but not being able to agree with him about the price, to spite Donatello they gave it to Nanni, who promised to take whatever they would give him. But when the statue was finished and set up, he asked a greater price than Donatello had asked. The consuls of the guild therefore turned again to Donatello, thinking that envy would make him estimate the value of the statue much lower than if it had been his work. But they were deceived, for Donatello gave judgment that more should be given to Nanni than he had asked. And they, not willing to agree to such a judgment, cried out to Donatello, "Why, if you would have done the work for less, do you value it more highly from the hand of another, and constrain us to pay more than he himself asks, and yet you acknowledge that it would have been better done if you had done it?" Donatello answered, laughing, "This good man is not as good at the art as I am, and suffers much more fatigue than I; therefore it appears to me that as just men you are bound to pay him for the time that he has spent." So his decision was accepted, the two parties having agreed to abide by it.

Below the niche in which it was placed are four saints in marble, made by Nanni for the guilds of the smiths, carpenters, and masons. It is said that when they were all finished he found that it was not possible to get more than three into the niche, he having made some of them extending their arms. Then in despair he came to Donatello and prayed him to advise him how to repair his mistake. Donatello, laughing at the state of the case, said, "If you will promise to pay for a supper for me and my lads I will undertake to make the saints go into the niche without any trouble." Nanni then, having given the promise very readily, Donatello sent him to take some measures at Prato, and to do some other matters that would take a few days. And when he was gone, Donatello, with all his pupils and workmen, set to work and cut off from the statues here a shoulder and there the arms, making them fit in close together, with the hand of one appearing over the next one's shoulder. So Donatello having linked them together to conceal Nanni's mistake, they remain as tokens of concord and brotherly kindness ; while those who know nothing of the matter would never perceive the error. Nanni, on his return, finding that Donatello had rectified his mistake, gave him infinite thanks, and most willingly paid for the supper.

CHAPTER VII.

FRA GIOVANNI ANGELICO DA FIESOLE, whose secular name was Guido, deserves to be held in most honourable remembrance, both as an excellent painter and illuminator, and also as a perfect monk. He might have lived comfortably in the world, earning whatever he wished by his art, in which he excelled when still young, but being by nature good and serious, for his satisfaction and quiet, and also principally to save his soul, he entered the order of the Preaching Friars. There are in the convent of S. Marco in Florence some choir books illuminated by his hand, which are so. beautiful that nothing could be better, and some others like them, which he left at S. Domenico of Fiesole, painted with incredible patience. It is true that in these he was aided by an elder brother, who was also an illuminator and skilled in painting.

One of the first of this good father's paintings was in the Certosa of Florence, our Lady with the Child in her arms and angels at her feet singing and playing. He also painted in fresco in S. Maria Novella. He was so beloved by Cosimo de' Medici that when the church and convent of S. Marco were built, he caused him to paint in it all the Passion of Jesus Christ, with many of the saints. They say that for the figure of S. Cosimo Fra Giovanni drew from life his friend the sculptor, Nanni d'Antonio di Banco. Below he painted S. Domenic at the foot of a tree, and in medallions among the branches all the popes, cardinals, bishops, saints, and doctors who had belonged to the order of the Preaching Friars. In these the friars aided him by sending to different places and obtaining portraits from life.

He also painted a picture for the high altar of S. Domenico of Fiesole, but this has been retouched by other masters and injured; but other pictures there by him have been better preserved, and there are a number of little figures in celestial glory, which are so beautiful that they seem really in Paradise, and no one who sees them can ever weary of looking at them. But beyond all that Fra Giovanni ever did is a painting in the same church of the Coronation of the Virgin in the midst of a choir of angels and an infinite number of saints, which it gives one a wonderful pleasure to look at, for it seems as if blessed spirits could look no otherwise in heaven, at least if they had bodies, and they are all so life-like and so sweet; and the whole colouring also of the work seems to be from the hand of a saint or

an angel, so that it was with good reason that he
was always called Fra Giovanni Angelico.

By so many works the name of Fra Giovanni
became famous in all Italy, and Pope Nicholas V.
sent for him, and made him paint the chapel of the
palace where the Pope hears mass, and also illumi-
nate some books, which are most beautiful. And
because Fra Giovanni seemed to the Pope, as he was
indeed, a man of most holy life, quiet and modest,
when the archbishopric of Florence fell vacant, he
adjudged him worthy of the rank; but the friar
hearing of it prayed his Holiness to give it to another,
because he did not feel himself apt at governing men,
and that his order had another friar loving to the
poor, learned, skilled in government, and Godfearing,
whom the dignity would much better become than it
would him. The Pope hearing this, and perceiving
that what he said was true, granted him the favour,
and so Fra Antonino, of the order of Preaching
Friars, was made Archbishop of Florence, a man of
such holiness that he was canonized by Adrian VI.
in our days. And this great goodness of Fra
Giovanni was in truth a rare thing, thus to give up
a dignity and honour offered him to one whom in
sincerity of heart he judged more worthy of it than
himself. And would to God that all religious men
would spend their time as this truly angelical father
did, in the service of God and to the benefit of the
world and their neighbours. Fra Giovanni was a

SAINTS ADORING. By FRA ANGELICO.

simple man and most holy in his habits, and one day
when Pope Nicholas V. desired him to dine with
him, he had scruples of conscience about eating
meat without his prior's leave, not considering the
Pope's authority. He would not follow the ways of
the world, but lived purely and holily, and was a
great friend of the poor. He painted constantly, and
would never represent anything but the saints. He
might have been rich, but did not care about it, saying that true riches are nothing else than being content with little. He might have governed many, and
would not, saying it was less troublesome to obey, and
one was less liable to err in obeying. It was in his
power to hold dignities among the friars and elsewhere, but he did not esteem them, affirming that
he sought no other dignity than to escape hell and
attain to paradise. He was most kind and sober,
keeping himself free from all worldly ties, often saying that he who practised art had need of quiet and
to be able to live without cares, and that he who
represents the things of Christ should always live
with Christ. He was never seen in anger by the
friars, which is a great thing, and seems to me
almost impossible to believe; and he had a way of
admonishing his friends with smiles. To those who
sought his works he would answer, that they must
content the prior, and then he would not fail. To
sum up, this father, who can never be enough
praised, was in all his works and words most humble

and modest, and in his paintings facile and devout ; and the saints whom he painted have more the air and likeness of saints than those of any one else. It was his habit never to retouch or alter any of his paintings, but to leave them as they came the first time, believing, as he said, that such was the will of God. Some say he would never take up his pencil until he had first made supplication, and he never made a crucifix but he was bathed in tears.

CHAPTER VIII.

ANTONELLO DA MESSINA, ANDREA DAL CASTAGNO, AND DOMENICO VENEZIANO.

FROM the time of Cimabue pictures either on panel or canvas had been painted in distemper, although the artists felt that a certain softness and freshness was wanting. But although many had sought for some other method, none had been able to find any-thing good, either by using liquid varnishes, or by mixing the colours in any other way. They could not find any way by which pictures on panels could be made durable like those on the walls, and could be washed without losing the colour. And though many times artists had assembled to discuss the matter, it had been in vain. This same desire was felt also by painters out of Italy, in France, Spain, and Germany, and elsewhere. It happened therefore while matters were in this state that John of Bruges,[1] a painter much esteemed in Flanders, set himself to try various kinds of colours and different oils to make varnishes,

---

[1] Johann van Eyck.

7

being one who delighted in alchemy. For having once taken great pains in painting a picture, when he had brought it to a conclusion with great care, he put on the varnish and put it to dry in the sun, as is usual. But either the heat was too great or the wood not seasoned enough, for the panel opened at all the joints. Upon which John, seeing the harm that the heat of the sun had done, determined to do something so that the sun should not spoil any more of his works. And he began to consider whether he could not find a varnish that should dry in the shade without having to put his pictures in the sun. He made many experiments, and at last found that the oil of linseed and the oil of nuts were the best for drying of all that he tried. Having boiled them with his other mixtures, he made the varnish that he, or rather all the painters of the world, had been so long desiring. He saw also that when the colours were mixed with these oils, not only were they safe from injury by water when once they were dry, but the colours also had more lustre without the aid of any varnish, and besides, which seemed more marvellous to him, the colours blended better than in tempera.

The fame of this invention soon spread not only through Flanders, but to Italy and many other parts of the world, and great desire was aroused in other artists to know how he brought his works to such perfection. And seeing his pictures, and not knowing how they were done, they were obliged to give him great praise, while at the same time they envied him with a virtuous envy, especially because for a time he would not let any one see him work, or teach any one his secret. But when he was grown old he at last favoured Roger of Bruges, his pupil, with the knowledge, and Roger taught others. But although the merchants bought the paintings and sent them to princes and other great personages to their great profit, the thing was not known beyond Flanders. The pictures, however, especially when they were new, had that strong smell which mixing oil with colours gives them, so that it would seem the secret might have been discovered; but for many years it was not.

It came about then that some Florentines who traded in Flanders and Naples sent a picture containing many figures painted in oil by John to King Alfonso I. of Naples, and the picture pleasing him from the beauty of the figures and the new method of colouring, all the painters in the kingdom came together to see it, and it was highly praised by all.

Now there was a certain Antonello da Messina, a man of an acute mind and well skilled in his art, who had studied drawing at Rome for many years, and afterwards worked at Palermo, and finally came back to Messina, his native place, and had obtained a good repute for his skill in painting. He, going on business from Sicily to Naples, heard that this picture by

John of Bruges had come from Flanders to the King Alfonso, and that it could be washed, and was altogether perfect. He contrived therefore to see it, and the vivacity of the colours, and the way in which they were blended, had such an effect upon him that, laying aside all other matters, he set off for Flanders. And when he came to Bruges he presented himself to John, and made him many presents of drawings in the Italian manner, and other things, so that John, moved by these and the deference Antonello paid him, and feeling himself growing old, allowed Antonello to see his method of painting in oil, and he did not leave the place until he had learnt all that he desired. But when John was dead Antonello returned to his country to make Italy participate in his useful and convenient secret. And after having spent some months in Messina he went to Venice, where, being a person much given to pleasure, he determined to settle and end his days. There he painted many pictures in oil, and acquired a great name.

Among the other painters of name who were then in Venice, the chief was a Master Domenico. He received Antonello when he came to Venice with as much attention and courtesy as if he were a very dear friend. Antonello therefore, not to be outdone in courtesy, after a little while taught him the secret of painting in oil. No act of courtesy or kindness could have been more pleasing to him, for it caused him to gain lasting honour in his native place.

Now although emulation and honest rivalry are things praiseworthy and to be held in esteem, being necessary and useful to the world, envy, which cannot endure that another should have praise and honour, deserves the utmost scorn and reproach, as may be seen in the story of the unhappy Andrea dal Castagno, who, great as he was in painting and design, was greater still in the hatred and envy that he bore to other painters, so that the shadow of his sin has hidden the splendour of his talents. He was born at a small farm called Castagno, from which he took his surname when he came to live in Florence. Having been left an orphan in his childhood, he was taken by his uncle and employed by him many years in keeping cattle. While at such work it happened one day that to escape the rain he took refuge in a place where one of those country painters who work for little pay was painting a countryman's tabernacle. Andrea, who had never seen anything like it before, excited by curiosity, set himself to watch and to consider the manner of such work, and there awoke within him suddenly such a strong desire and passionate longing for art that without loss of time he began to draw little figures and animals in charcoal, and carve them with the point of a knife on the walls or the stones, so as to excite no little marvel in those who saw them. The fame of this new study of Andrea's spread among the country people, and, as fortune would have it, it came to the ears of a

Florentine gentleman, named Bernardetto de' Medici, who had land in those parts, and he desired to see the boy. And having heard him talk with much quickness and intelligence, he asked him if he would like to be a painter. And Andrea answering that there was nothing he desired more, he took him with him to Florence, and placed him with one of the masters who were at that time held to be the best. So Andrea giving himself to study showed great intelligence in overcoming the difficulties of the art. His colour was somewhat crude, but he was excellent in the movement of figures and in the heads both of men and women. One picture of his which excited the astonishment of artists was a fresco of the Flagellation, which would be the finest of all his works if it had not been so scratched and spoiled by children and simple people, who destroyed the heads and arms of the Jews to avenge, as it were, the injury done to the Lord.

Afterwards he was charged to paint a part of the larger chapel of S. Maria Nuova, another part being given to Alesso Baldovinetti, and a third to Domenico da Venezia, who had been brought to Florence on account of his new method of painting in oil. Then Andrea was seized with envy of Domenico, for although he knew himself to be more excellent than he in drawing, yet he could not bear that a foreigner should be caressed and honoured in such a manner by the citizens, and his rage and anger grew so hot

that he began to think how he could rid himself of
him. Nevertheless, Andrea was as clever in dis·
simulation as he was in painting, and could assume
a cheerful countenance whenever he liked; he was
ready in speech, proud, resolute in mind and in
every movement of his body. Being jealous of
others as well as of Domenico, he used secretly to
scratch their paintings. Even in his youth, if any
one found fault with his works, he would let him
know by blows or insults that he knew how to
defend himself from injury.

But now resolving to do by treachery what he
could not do openly without manifest danger, he
feigned great friendship for this Domenico, and he
being a good fellow and amiable, fond of singing
and playing the lute, willingly made friends with
him, Andrea appearing to be both a man of talent
and good company. And this friendship continuing,
on one side real and on the other feigned, every night
they were found together enjoying themselves, and
serenading their loves, which Domenico much
delighted in. He also loving Andrea truly, taught
him how to paint in oils, which was not yet known
in Tuscany.

Meanwhile, in the chapel of S. Maria Nuova,
Andrea painted the Annunciation, which is considered very fine; and on the other side Domenico
painted in oils S. Joachim and S. Anna and the
birth of our Lady, and below the Betrothal of the

Virgin, with a good number of portraits from life:
Bernardetto de' Medici, constable of the Florentines,
in a red cap, Bernardo Guadagni, the gonfalonier,
Folco Portinari, and others of that family. But this
work was left unfinished, as will be seen. Andrea,
on his side, painted in oils the death of the Virgin,
and showed that he knew how to manage oil colours
as well as Domenico his rival. In this picture also
he put many portraits from life, and in a circle himself like Judas Iscariot, as he was in truth and deed.

Then having brought this work to a successful
termination, blinded by envy at the praises he heard
given to Domenico, he meditated how to rid himself
of him; and having thought of many ways, he at last
proceeded in this manner. One evening in summer,
Domenico as usual took his lute and departed from
S. Maria Nuova, leaving Andrea in his chamber
drawing, he having refused to accompany him on
the excuse of having to make certain drawings of
importance. So Domenico being gone out to his
pleasure, Andrea disguised himself and went to wait
for him at the corner, and when Domenico came up,
returning home, he struck at him with a leaden
instrument, and breaking his lute, pierced him in
the stomach at the same moment. But thinking
he had not done his work as he wished, he struck
him on the head heavily, and leaving him on the
ground, returned to his room in S. Maria Nuova, and
sat down to his drawing as Domenico had left him.

In the meantime the servants, having heard a noise, ran out and heard what had happened, and came running to bring the evil tidings to Andrea, the traitor and murderer, whereupon he ran to the place where lay Domenico, and could not be consoled, crying out without ceasing, "Oh, my brother, my brother!" At last Domenico died in his arms, and it could not be found out who it was that had slain him. Nor would it ever have been known, if Andrea on his deathbed had not made confession of the deed.

He lived in honour; but spending much, particularly on his dress and in his manner of living, he left little wealth behind him. When Giuliano de' Medici was slain, and his brother Lorenzo wounded, by the Pazzi and their adherents, the Signory resolved that the conspirators should be painted as traitors on the façade of the palace of the Podestà. And the work being offered to Andrea, he accepted it willingly, being much beholden to the house of Medici. He painted it surprisingly well, and it would be impossible to describe how much art he displayed in the portraits, painted for the most part from the men themselves, representing them hanging by their feet in all sorts of strange attitudes. The work pleased the people so much that from that time he was called no more Andrea dal Castagno, but Andrea degli Impiccati, Andrea of the hanged men.

CHAPTER IX.

FILIPPO LIPPI AND BOTTICELLI.

FRA FILIPPO DI TOMMASO LIPPI was born in Florence in a street called Ardiglione, behind the convent of the Carmelite fathers. By the death of Tommaso his father he was left an orphan when a poor little boy of two years old, his mother having died at his birth. He remained with his aunt until he was eight years old, when, being no longer able to support him, she made him a Carmelite friar. In the convent, although he was clever and dexterous with his fingers, he showed himself stupid at his letters, and would never apply his mind to learning. For the boy, who was still called by the name of Filippo, instead of studying while he was in his noviciate and under the discipline of the grammar master, did nothing but cover his books with drawings of figures, until at last the prior determined to give him every help in learning to paint. The chapel in the Carmine had been recently painted by Masaccio, and being most beautiful, pleased Fra Filippo greatly, and he used to go there every day

for his recreation. Working there in company with
the many other youths who were always drawing
there, he surpassed them greatly both in knowledge
and skill, so that it was considered certain that he
would do something wonderful in time. But even
in his tender years he did something so good that it
was marvellous; for he painted a pope confirming
the rule of the Carmelites and other pictures so
much in Masaccio's style that many said that the
spirit of Masaccio had entered into Fra Filippo.

Finding himself thus praised by every one, at the
age of seventeen he threw off the cowl. And going
to Ancona, he was disporting himself one day with
some of his friends in a boat in the sea, when they
were all captured by some Moorish ships that were
scouring the bay, and carried off to Barbary, where
they were chained as slaves. In this condition, in
much suffering, he remained for eighteen months, but
being much with his master, it came into his head
one day to make his portrait, and taking a piece
of charcoal out of the fire, he drew him at full length
on the white wall in his Moorish dress. The other
slaves told his master what he had done, and he
thought it was a miracle, neither drawing nor
painting being known in those parts, and this was
the cause of his being set free from captivity. For
having completed some works in colour for his
master, he was conducted in safety to Naples,
whence he soon returned to Florence. He was

taken into great favour by Cosimo de' Medici, but being devoted to pleasure, he neglected his work for it. Cosimo therefore, when he was working for him in his house, caused him to be shut in, so that he could not go out and waste his time; but he, cutting up the sheets of the bed with a pair of scissors, made a rope and let himself down by the window. When after many days he returned to his work, Cosimo gave him his liberty, considering the peril he had run, and sought to keep him for the future by many favours, and so he served him more readily, saying that genius is a heavenly being, and not a beast of burden.

While he was painting for the nuns of S. Margherita, he saw one day the daughter of Francesco Buti, a Florentine citizen, who was there either as a boarder or a novice. Fra Filippo seeing Lucrezia, who was very beautiful, persuaded the nuns to let him paint her for the figure of our Lady. And falling in love with her, he contrived when she was going to see the girdle of our Lady, the chief relic of the place, to carry her away. The nuns were much distressed at it, and Francesco her father was never happy again, and did all he could to recover her, but she would not return.

Sandro Botticelli was a disciple of his, and his own son Filippo was also a painter of fine genius. After his father's death, being then very young, he became Sandro Botticelli's pupil, though his father in dying had commended him to Fra Diamante his friend, almost his brother. He was a man of great talent, copious invention in ornament, and introduced new methods of varying the dresses, attiring many of his figures in antique garments. He made great use of ancient Roman vases, trophies, armour, swords, togas, and other such things. And when he died he was wept by all who had known him, not only for his excellence in his art, but for his good life and his courteous and amiable disposition.

It was in the time of the magnificent Lorenzo de' Medici, which was indeed an age of gold for men of genius, that that Alessandro flourished who was nicknamed according to our custom Sandro di Botticello. He was the son of a Florentine citizen, Mariano Filipepi, and was carefully taught all that it was usual to teach children in those times before they were apprenticed; but though he learnt readily all he wished, he was restless and discontented, so that his father, wearied with his fancies, placed him in despair with one of his acquaintances, a goldsmith named Botticello. There was at that time great intimacy and continual intercourse between the goldsmiths and the painters, and Sandro, attracted by painting, determined to take to it. His father learning his wish, took him therefore to Fra Filippo and placed him with him to learn his art. Giving himself to study, he followed his master so closely that he won Fra Filippo's affection, and was so well instructed by him as to rise rapidly to unexpected success.   Having made himself a reputation, he was employed to paint in S. Marco, and did many things in the house of Lorenzo de' Medici, especially a Pallas as large as life, and a Sebastian.   He painted also in many houses in the city, and among them are a bust of Venus and another Venus whom the Graces deck with flowers denoting the spring.

In S. Pietro Maggiore he made a picture for Matteo Palmieri with an infinite number of figures.   This is the Assumption of our Lady, with the Zones of the heavens, the Patriarchs, Prophets, Apostles, Evangelists, Martyrs, Confessors, Doctors, and Hierarchies, according to the design given him by Matteo Palmieri, and this work he painted in a masterly manner and with infinite diligence.   At the foot of the picture are Matteo and his wife kneeling.   But although this work is most beautiful and ought to have overcome envy, some evil-minded persons, not able to find any other fault, said that Matteo and Sandro were guilty of grave heresy, which, whether it be true or not, is not for me to judge.   It is enough that Sandro deserves praise for his labours and the skill with which he represents the circles of the heavens, and for the foreshortening of the figures of the angels and their various postures, and all well carried out with good drawing.

About this time there was given to Sandro to paint a little picture to be placed in S. Maria Novella,

between the two doors. This is the Adoration of
the Magi, and you may notice the first old man
kissing the feet of our Lord and overcome with
tender emotion at the consummation of his long
journey. The figure of this king is the portrait of
old Cosimo de' Medici, the most lifelike and most
natural to be found in our days. The second king
is Giuliano de' Medici, the father of Clement VII.,
who may be seen intent on offering devout reverence
to the Child, and presenting his gift. The third,
who is kneeling and appears to be adoring Him and
confessing Him the true Messiah, is Giovanni, son
of Cosimo.

By such works, therefore, having made a name,
Pope Sixtus IV. sent for him to come to him. He
had built the chapel in his palace at Rome, and
desired to have it adorned with paintings. He appointed Sandro master of the works, and there he
painted many things, by which he gained among his
fellow-workers, both from Florence and other cities,
fame and a great name. He received from the Pope
a good sum of money, but this being soon consumed
by living improvidently, as was his custom, and the
work assigned him being finished, he returned to
Florence. Being fond of sophistry, he made a com-
mentary on Dante, and made illustrations for the
Inferno and engraved them, spending much time
upon them. He also engraved many of his designs,
but in a bad manner, the best from his hand being

the triumph of the faith of Fra Girolamo Savonarola
of Ferrara, of whose sect he was such a strong
partisan that he gave up painting. As he had no
means of his own, this threw him into great difficulties, but adhering obstinately to that party, and
becoming, as they called it, a Piagnone, he gave up
working, so that at last he found himself old and
poor; and if Lorenzo de' Medici while he lived, and
after him other of his friends, had not remembered
him, he would have died of hunger.

Sandro was a very amusing person and fond of
playing tricks on his pupils and friends. There is a
story that he had a pupil named Biagio, who copied
a round picture of his master's, representing the
Madonna with angels round her, for sale, and Sandro
sold it for him to a citizen for six gold florins.
Meeting Biagio afterwards he said to him, " I have
sold your picture at last, so to-night you must hang
it where it will be better seen, and to-morrow go and
fetch the man and bring him here that he may see it
well, then he will pay the money." " Oh, how well
you have done, master!" said Biagio; and going to
the workshop he hung the picture up and went away.
Then Sandro and Jacopo, another of his pupils,
made of paper eight red caps, such as the citizens
of Florence wear, and fixed them with some white
wax on the heads of the eight angels round the
Madonna in the picture. The next morning Biagio
appears, bringing with him the man who had bought

the picture, and who knew all about the trick. And coming in, Biagio raised his eyes and saw his Madonna, not in the midst of the angels, but sitting in the midst of the Signory of Florence; and he was about to cry out and to begin to excuse himself to the purchaser, when he perceived that he was silent and only praised the picture, so he remained silent also. At last Biagio going with the man to his house received his six florins as his master had agreed, and returned to the workshop. Meanwhile Sandro and Jacopo had taken off the caps, and he saw his angels were angels, and not citizens in caps. Altogether stupefied he knew not what to say, but at last turning to Sandro, he cried, " Master, I do not know whether I am dreaming, or whether it was true. These angels when I came in had red caps on their heads, and now they have not; what does it mean ? " " You are out of your mind, Biagio," answered Sandro. " This money has sent you mad. If it had been so do you think the man would have bought it ? " " That is true," answered Biagio, " he said nothing about it ; it seemed to me strange all the time." And all the other boys came round him and talked till they made him believe he had been off his head.

A cloth weaver came at one time to live next door to Sandro, and set up eight looms, which when they were at work not only deafened poor Sandro with the noise of the treadles, but also shook the house, so that there was no wall strong enough to stand it,

8

and with one thing and the other it was impossible to work or to stay in the house. He asked his neighbour many times to put a stop to this annoyance, but he only answered that in his own house he could and would do what pleased him. Then Sandro getting angry, set up on his wall, which was higher than his neighbour's, and not very strong, a huge stone, poised so that every time the wall shook it seemed to be just about to fall and crush the roof and beams and the looms of his neighbour. The man, alarmed at the danger, came running to Sandro, but he gave him answer in his own words, that in his own house he could and would do whatever pleased him; and the weaver could get no other answer, until at last he was forced to come to terms, and be a better neighbour to Sandro.

It is said that he held in high honour those whom he knew to be studious in art, and that he earned much himself, but from want of management and carelessness things went wrong. When he was old he became infirm, and used to go about with two sticks, not being able to stand upright; and so he died at the age of seventy-eight, and was buried in Ogni Santi in Florence, in the year 1515.

CHAPTER X.

THERE are some unhappy men who, after labouring by their studies to help others and to leave a memory of themselves, are prevented by infirmity or death from bringing their work to perfection. And often it happens that their works left thus unfinished are appropriated by others, who seek thus to hide their ass's hide under the lion's skin. So it befel Piero della Francesca dal Borgo S. Sepolcro, who being a great master in perspective, arithmetic, and geometry, was prevented by blindness in his old age from bringing to light the books he had written. And he who ought to have used all his powers in winning for him glory and a great name, having learnt all he knew from him, sought to conceal the name of Piero his preceptor, and usurped his honour, by publishing under his own name, that of Fra Luca dal Borgo, the good old man's works.

Piero was born in Borgo S. Sepolcro, now a city, but not so at that time, and he was called della

Francesca after his mother, because his father was dead before he was born, and it was she who brought him up, and aided him to attain to the rank he reached. Piero studied mathematics in his youth, and although from the age of fifteen he became a painter, he never gave up his mathematical studies, and his productions brought him so much credit that he was employed by the Duke of Urbino, and left in that place many of his writings on geometry and perspective, which are inferior to none of his time.

Afterwards being fetched to Rome by Nicolas V., he painted in his palace two pictures, which were afterwards destroyed by Pope Julius II., that Raffaello might paint there the imprisonment of S. Peter. Thence he went to Loreto, and painted there in company with Domenico Veneziano; but the plague breaking out, he left his work unfinished, and it was afterwards completed by Luca of Cortona his pupil. From Loreto he went to Arezzo, where he painted the whole history of the Cross, from the time when the sons of Adam laying him in the tomb placed under his tongue the seeds of the tree from which the cross sprang, to the exaltation of the Cross by the Emperor Heraclius.

Piero was, as we have said, most studious in his art, and had a good knowledge of Euclid, so that Maestro Luca dal Borgo who wrote on geometry was his pupil. Lorentino d' Angelo was also his pupil, and finished the works that he left incomplete

at his death.   There is a story told of this Lorentino
that once when the carnival was near his children
kept begging him to kill a pig, as the custom was in
those parts.   Then, remembering that he had no
money, they said, "What will father do to buy the
pig without money?"   To which he replied, "Some
saint will help us."   But when he had said this
many times and no pig appeared, their hopes began
to fail.   But at last there came a countryman who,
to fulfil a vow, wanted a S. Martin painted, but had
nothing to give for the picture but a pig that was
worth five lire.   When Lorentino heard this he said
he would paint the picture, and would take nothing
but the pig for it.   Lorentino painted the saint, and
the countryman brought the pig, and so the saint
provided the pig for his poor children.

Piero Perugino was also his pupil, but the one who
did him most honour was Luca Signorelli of Cortona.
For Luca Signorelli was in his time as famous a
painter in Italy as any one has ever been.   While
he worked in Arezzo with Piero, dwelling in the
house of Lazzaro Vasari his uncle, he imitated the
manner of Piero his master, so that one could be hardly
known from the other.   His first works were in
Arezzo, where he painted in many churches.   There
is a S. Michael weighing souls, which is admirable,
and in which may be seen his power in painting the
splendour of arms with all the reflections of light.
Having come to Florence to see the works of the

masters there, he painted on a canvas some of the old gods, which were much admired, and a picture of our Lady, and presented them both to Lorenzo, who would never be surpassed by any one in magnificent liberality.

In the principal church of Orvieto he completed the chapel begun by Fra Giovanni da Fiesole, painting the story of the end of the world with a strange and fantastical imagination; with angels, demons, earthquakes, fire, and ruin, together with many beautiful figures, and essaying to represent the terror of the last tremendous day. So that I do not marvel that Luca's works were always highly praised by Michael Angelo, nor that some things in his own divine Judgment were taken in part from Luca, such as angels, demons, the order of the heavens, and other things in which he imitated him, as any one can see.

It is told of him that when one of his sons whom he loved much was killed at Cortona, being very beautiful in face and form, Luca in the midst of his grief set himself with great constancy to paint his portrait, shedding no tears, nor giving way to grief, that he might always see through the work of his hands him whom nature had given to him and adverse fortune taken from him.

At last, having produced works for almost all the princes of Italy, he returned to Cortona, where in his last years he worked rather for pleasure than

SOLDIERS. By LUCA SIGNORELLI.

anything else. Thus in his old age he painted a
picture for the nuns of Santa Margherita in Arezzo,
and another for the company of S. Girolamo, which
was borne from Cortona to Arezzo on the shoulders
of men of the company. Luca, old as he was, came
to put it up, desiring also to see again his friends and
relations. He lodged in the house of the Vasari,
when I was then a little boy of eight years old, and
I remember how the good old man, who was very
courteous and gracious, having heard from the
master who gave me my first instruction that I
attended to nothing at school but drawing figures, I
remember, I say, how he turned to Antonio, my
father, and said, "Antonio, let Giorgino learn to
draw by all means, for even if later he takes to
literature, drawing will still be of use and honour
and profit to him, as it is to all men." Then turning
to me, who was standing in front of him, he said,
"Study, little kinsman," adding many other things
of which I will say nothing, because I know I have
not confirmed the opinion which the good old man
had of me. When he heard that I suffered from
nose-bleeding to such a degeee that I was often left
half dead, he hung a piece of jasper round my neck
with great tenderness of manner, and this remembrance of Luca is for ever fixed in my mind.

So having put the picture in its place, he returned
to Cortona, accompanied for a great distance by
many of the citizens and of his friends and relatives.

CHAPTER XI.

DOMENICO DI TOMMASO DEL GHIRLANDAJO was put by his father to his own art of a goldsmith. Tommaso had been the first to make those ornaments for the head which are worn by Florentine girls, and which are called garlands, whence he acquired the name of Ghirlandajo. But although Domenico was a goldsmith he was continually drawing, and became so quick and ready at it, that many say he could draw a likeness of any one who passed the shop; and this is the more readily to be believed as there are in his works a great number of lifelike portraits.

Having brought himself into notice by his works, he was employed by Francesco Sassetti to paint a chapel with the story of S. Francesco, in which he introduced among many other noted citizens the magnificent Lorenzo de' Medici. Afterwards he was called to Rome to help in the painting of the Sistine Chapel, and while there was employed by Francesco

Tornabuoni in painting the wall round the tomb of his wife which Andrea Verrocchio made. He painted here four pictures, with which Francesco was so pleased that when Domenico returned to Florence, he recommended him by letter to Giovanni, one of his relatives. When Giovanni heard it, he began to wish to employ him upon some magnificent work which would bring honour to his own memory and fame to Domenico. And at that time it happened that the principal chapel in S. Maria Novella, which had been painted by Andrea Orcagna, through a fault in the roof, had been spoilt by water. Many of the citizens had been wishing to have it restored or repainted, but the owners, being the Ricci, would not agree, not being able to bear the expense themselves, and not willing that others should do it, lest they should lose their rights and their arms should be taken down. Giovanni, desiring to give it to Domenico to paint, set himself to obtain leave in some way or other, and at last promised the Ricci to bear all the expense himself, and to put their arms in the most conspicuous and honourable place in the chapel. So, having come to terms, and a contract being drawn up of very strict tenour, Giovanni set Domenico to work, the price to be twelve hundred ducats of gold, and if the work pleased him two hundred more.

So Domenico set to work and never rested till he had finished it in four years, which was in 1485, to the very great satisfaction of this Giovanni, who allowèd that he had been well served, and confessed ingenuously that Domenico had earned the two hundred ducats extra, but said it would give him pleasure if he would be content with the first sum ; and Domenico, who loved glory more than riches, gave up the remainder at once, saying he cared more to satisfy him than to have the money.

Then Giovanni had two great coats-of-arms made in stone, one of the Tornaquinci family and the other of the Tornabuoni, and set them up on piers outside the chapel, and in the arch, besides other arms of the same family with different names and different shields, the Giachinotti, Popoleschi, Marabottini, and Cardinali. And when Domenico made the altar-piece under an arch in the gilded ornament of the picture, he had a very beautiful tabernacle for the Sacrament made, and in the front of it he put a little shield blazoned with the arms of the Ricci. And the best of it was at the opening of the chapel, for the Ricci having sought with a great outcry for their arms, not being able to find them, went to the magistrates, taking the contract with them. But the Tornabuoni showed that their arms had been placed in the most conspicuous and the most honourable place in the chapel, and though they exclaimed that they could not be seen, they were told that they were wrong, and that as they had been placed in the most honourable place, near to the Holy Sacrament, they must be content.   And so it was decided by the magistrates.

For the same Giovanni Tornabuoni Domenico painted a chapel in his house a little way from the city.   He was so fond of work and so anxious to please every one that he used to tell his scholars to take any commission that was brought to the shop, if it were only the hoops for women's petticoat paniers, for if they would not do them he would paint them himself, rather than that any one should go away from his shop discontented.   He disliked greatly any domestic cares, and therefore left all the management to his brother David, saying, " Let me work and you see about providing everything, for now that I have begun to understand the methods of the art, I am sorry that they have not given me the whole circuit of the walls of Florence to paint."   They say that when he was drawing the antiquities at Rome, arches, columns, coliseums, and amphitheatres, he did it all by eye, without rule or measurement. Drawing the Coliseum in this way, he put at the foot of it a figure erect, by measuring which you can find the measurement of the whole building, for, being tried by capable men after his death, it was found correct.

He painted some things at the Abbey of Passignano belonging to the monks of Vallombrosa, together with his brother David and Bastiano da S. Gimignano.   Before the arrival of Domenico, the painters

found themselves very ill entertained by the monks,
so they requested the abbot to serve them better,
saying it was not fair to treat them like labourers.
The abbot promised to do so, and excused himself
saying it came from ignorance and not malice. But
Domenico came, and all went on in the same way,
so David, going to the abbot again, said he came
not on his own account, but because of his brother's
worth and talents. The abbot being however an
ignorant man, made a similar reply. In the evening,
as they sat down to supper, the monk who had the
charge of the strangers, came bringing a board with
porringers and food fit only for coarse people just as
before, upon which David, springing up in a rage,
flung the soup over the friar's back, and taking up the
loaf from the table attacked him with it, and struck
him so fiercely that he was carried half dead to his
cell. The abbot, who was already in bed, hearing
the noise, sprang up and came out, thinking the
monastery was falling into ruins, and finding the
friar in bad case began to reproach David. But he
being infuriated bade him take himself off, for his
brother Domenico was worth more than all the
pigs of abbots that ever were in that monastery.
And from that time the abbot took pains to treat
them as they ought to have been treated.

Domenico had a pupil named Jacopo l' Indaco,
who was a reasonably good master in his time. It
is not strange that few works left his hands, for he

was a merry, idle fellow, and would never work if he could help it. He used to say it was not a Christian thing to do nothing but labour and take no pleasure. He was very intimate with Michael Angelo, and that great artist when he wanted recreation, after his great labours of mind and body, could find no one more to his humour. And because he found pleasure in his chatter and his jokes, he used to have him constantly to dine with him. But one day his company becoming wearisome, as such people generally do become to their friends by continually chattering without discretion and at wrong times, Michael Angelo, to get rid of him, having something else to do, sent him out to buy some figs. And as soon as Jacopo was out of the house he fastened the door behind him, determined not to let him in when he came back. So when l' Indaco came back from the market and found, after knocking at the door in vain for some time, that Michael Angelo would not open it, he took the figs and the leaves in which they were wrapped and strewed them all over the threshold. Then he went away, and for many months he would not speak to Michael Angelo, and though they afterwards made it up, they were never such friends as before.

Cosimo Rosselli was called to Rome at the same time as Domenico Ghirlandajo to paint in the Sistine Chapel, and there, working in company with Sandro Botticelli, Luca da Cortona, and Piero Perugino, he

painted three pictures. There is a story told that
the Pope had offered a prize to the painter who, according to the Pope's own judgment, should work
best. When the pictures were finished, his Holiness
went to see them, every painter having done his
utmost to deserve the reward. Cosimo, knowing
himself to be weak in invention and design, had
sought to hide his defects by covering his picture
with the finest ultramarine and other bright colours,
and there was not a tree, or a blade of grass, or a
garment, or a cloud that was not shining with gold,
for he thought that the Pope, understanding little of
art, would give him the prize on that account.
When the day was come that all their works were
uncovered, and his was seen, it was received with
great laughter and many scoffing jests by the other
artists, who all mocked him without pity. But in
the end the laughter was turned against them, for,
as Cosimo had imagined, the colours dazzled the
eyes of the Pope, who did not much understand such
matters, although he took great pleasure in them,
and he decided that Cosimo had done much better
than all the others. And having given him the
prize, he commanded the others to cover their
pictures with the best azure that could be found,
and to touch them up with gold that they might be
like Cosimo's in colour and richness. So the poor
painters, filled with despair at having to satisfy the
Holy Father's small understanding, set themselves

TWO SAINTS. By COSIMO ROSSELLI.

to spoil all their good work, and Cosimo laughed at those who a little before had laughed at him.

He afterwards returned to Florence with a little money, and lived comfortably there, having as his pupil Piero, who was always called Piero di Cosimo.

This Piero was the son of one Lorenzo, a goldsmith, but is never known under any other name than Piero di Cosimo. His father seeing his inclination to drawing, gave him into Cosimo's care, who received him willingly, and loved him as his son; and always considered him as such. The boy had by nature a lofty spirit, being absent-minded and very different from the other boys who studied under Cosimo. He would get so intent on what he was doing that if a matter was being discussed it would sometimes be necessary to begin again, and relate the whole matter a second time, because his mind had gone away to something else. And he was so fond of solitude that he had no greater pleasure than going by himself to weave fancies and build castles in the air. His master Cosimo made great use of him, and could leave him to conduct matters of importance, knowing that Piero had a better manner and more judgment than himself. He took him with him to Rome when Pope Sixtus summoned him to work in his chapel, and in one of his pictures there Piero painted a most beautiful landscape. And because he drew well from nature he painted in Rome the portraits of many distinguished men.

After the death of Cosimo he shut himself up, and
would let no one see him work, living more like a
wild beast than a man. He would never have his
rooms swept, eat just when he felt hungry, would
not have his garden dug or the fruit trees pruned,
but let the vines grow and their branches trail on the
ground, and seemed to find pleasure in seeing everything as wild as his own nature, saying that things
of this sort ought to be left to nature to take care of.
He would often go to see any animal or plant that
was made strangely, and would talk of it until he
wearied his hearers.

He had seen some things of Lionardo's, finished
with the extreme care that Lionardo would take
when he wished to show his art, and this manner
pleasing Piero, he sought to imitate it, though he
was very far from attaining to Lionardo's skill, and
was unlike him; indeed, he may be said to have
changed his manner in almost everything he did. If
he had not been so abstracted, and had taken more
care of himself, he would have made his great genius
known, so that he would have been adored; whereas
he was generally held to be mad, though he did no
harm except perhaps to himself, and did good to his
art by his works.

I must not forget to say that Piero in his youth,
having a fantastic and strange invention, was often
employed in the masquerades at the carnival, and
was therefore much in favour with the noble Floren-

tine youths, greatly improving with his invention that pastime. Some say he was the first to turn them into a kind of triumphal procession; at any rate, he improved them, introducing music appropriate to the subjects represented, and adding great pompous processions of men and horses in suitable habits and costumes. And certainly it was a fine thing to see at night twenty-five or thirty pairs of horses, richly accoutred, with their masters attired according to the subject represented, six or eight attendants in livery following each cavalier, torch in hand, perhaps to the number of four hundred, and behind them the car with trophies and fantastical extravagances, all which things give great pleasure to the people. I will just touch briefly on one of his inventions in mature years, not because of its agreeableness, but, on the contrary, because by its strange and unexpected horror it gave no little pleasure to the people. This was the car of Death, made in such secresy in the hall of the Pope that no one was allowed to see it. It was a triumphal car, hung in black and painted with dead men's bones and white crosses, and drawn by buffaloes; and on the car was a great figure of Death with a scythe in his hand, and all round were tombs. At the places where the triumphal procession was used to stop to sing, the tombs opened and there came out figures dressed in black, on which were painted the bones of the skeleton, horrible to look at, and they sang to

9

the sound of muffled trumpets in melancholy music
that noble song—

"Dolor, pianto e penitenza," &c.

Before and after the car rode a great number of the
dead on horseback, singing in a trembling voice the
Miserere.

This spectacle, from its novelty, satisfied all, and
Piero, the author and inventor, was much praised
and commended.

I heard Andrea di Cosimo, and Andrea del Sarto,
his pupils, who aided him in the preparation, say
that it was the opinion of the time that it was intended to signify the return of the house of Medici,
for they were then exiles, or, as you may say, dead,
and were soon to rise again ; and so some of the
words of the song were interpreted.

None could paint horrible dragons better than he,
as may be seen from a sea mónster which he presented to the magnificent Giuliano de' Medici. This
monster is now in the Guardaroba of Duke Cosimo
de' Medici, where is also a book of animals of the
same kind, most beautiful and strange, and drawn
with the greatest patience. Indeed, in all his works
there is a spirit very different from that of others,
and a certain subtilty in investigating nature regardless of time or fatigue, only for his own pleasure.
And indeed it could not be otherwise, for enamoured
of nature, he cared not for his own comfort, but

brought himself to living on hard eggs, which, to
spare firing, he cooked when he boiled his varnishes,
not six or eight at once, but by fifties, keeping them
in a basket to consume by degrees. This sort of life
he enjoyed so much that he thought all other to be
mere slavery. He could not endure the crying of
children, the sound of coughing, the ringing of bells,
or the chanting of friars ; but when the skies were
pouring down rain he liked to see it rushing from
the roofs and streaming down the streets. He had
great fear of lightning, and when it thundered he
would wrap himself in his cloak, and shutting his
windows and the door of his room, would hide himself in a corner until it was over. His conversation
was so varied that sometimes he would say things
that would make people shake with laughing. But
with old age he grew more strange and fantastical,
and would not even have his pupils near him. He
wanted still to work, but could not, being paralyzed,
and in paroxysms of rage would try to force his hands
to keep steady, and would drop now his mahlstick,
and now his pencils, until it made one sad to see him.
The flies and even the shadows irritated him. He
would talk of the sufferings of those who have linger-
ing diseases, and would accuse physicians and nurses
of letting sick men die of hunger, besides torturing
them with syrups and medicines. He would say
that it was a fine thing to die by the hand of justice
in the open air, with many people round you, sup-

ported by good words, and having the priest and the
people praying for you, and going with the angels to
paradise.   In such strange talk and ways he lingered
on, till one morning he was found lying dead at the
foot of the stairs.

CHAPTER XII.

In the country of Prato, distant from Florence ten miles, at a village called Savignano, was born Bartolommeo, whose name according to Tuscan use was shortened into Baccio. Showing aptitude for drawing in his childhood, through the mediation of Benedetto da Maiano he was placed in Cosimo Rosselli's workshop, dwelling for many years with some of his relatives near the gate of S. Piero Gattolini, so that he was never known by any other name than Baccio della Porta. In the same workshop was Mariotto Albertinelli, who formed such a close intimacy with Baccio della Porta that they were one soul and one body, and there was such a brotherly friendship between them that when Baccio left Cosimo to practise his art by himself as a master, Mariotto went with him, and there at the gate of S. Piero Gattolini they lived, producing many works together. But as Mariotto was not so well grounded in drawing as Baccio, he gave himself to the study

of the antiquities that were then in Florence, the
greater number and the best of which were in the
house of the Medici.   For the garden there was full
of antique fragments, the study not of Mariotto
alone, but of all the sculptors and painters of his
time.   Mariotto profited greatly by the study of
these antiquities, and took service with Madonna
Alfonsina, the mother of Duke Lorenzo, who gave
him every assistance.   He drew Madonna Alfonsina
from life very well, and seemed to have found his
fortune by being admitted to her friendship.   But in
the year 1494, Piero de' Medici being banished, her
aid failed him, and he returned to the house of
Baccio, where he set himself to study from nature,
and to imitate Baccio's works, until in a little while
many mistook his paintings for Baccio's.

Baccio was much beloved in Florence, being as-
siduous at work, quiet, good-hearted, and God-fear-
ing.   A quiet life pleased him best; he avoided all
vicious habits, delighted in hearing preaching, and
sought the company of learned and grave persons.
At this time Fra Girolamo Savonarola from Ferrara,
the famous theologian of the order of Preaching
Friars, was at S. Mark's, and Baccio constantly
frequenting his preaching, came into close intercourse with him, and almost lived at the convent,
being joined in friendship with the other friars also.
And Fra Girolamo preaching constantly that evil
pictures and amorous books and music tempted

... artists that were then in Florence, the ... ... and the best of which were at the ... ... Florence. For the garden there was full ... ... fragments, the story not of Michael ... ... of all the sculptors and painters of ... ... Michael profited greatly by the study ... ... antiquities, and took service with Madonna ... ... the mother of Duke Lorenzo, who ... ... assistance. He drew Madonna Ages so ... from life very well, and seemed to have begun ... ... by being admitted to her friendship. Then in the year 1494, Piero de' Medici being banished ... ... failed him, and he returned to the house of Bertoldo, who told him off to study from nature, and to imitate Bertoldo's works, until in a little while many mistook his nature for Bertoldo's.

Bertoldo was much beloved in Florence, but a ... ... work, quiet, good-hearted, and God-fear... ... quiet life pleased him best; he avoided the ... ... delighted in hearing preached ... ... company of learned and grave persons ... ... Fra Girolamo Savonarola then ... ... the famous theologian of the order of Preaching friars, was at S. Mark's, and Bertoldo ... ... frequenting his preaching, came into close inter... ... with him, and almost lived at the convent ... ... in friendship with the other friars also ... ... this Girolamo preaching constantly that evil ... ... and amorous books, and music, tempt...

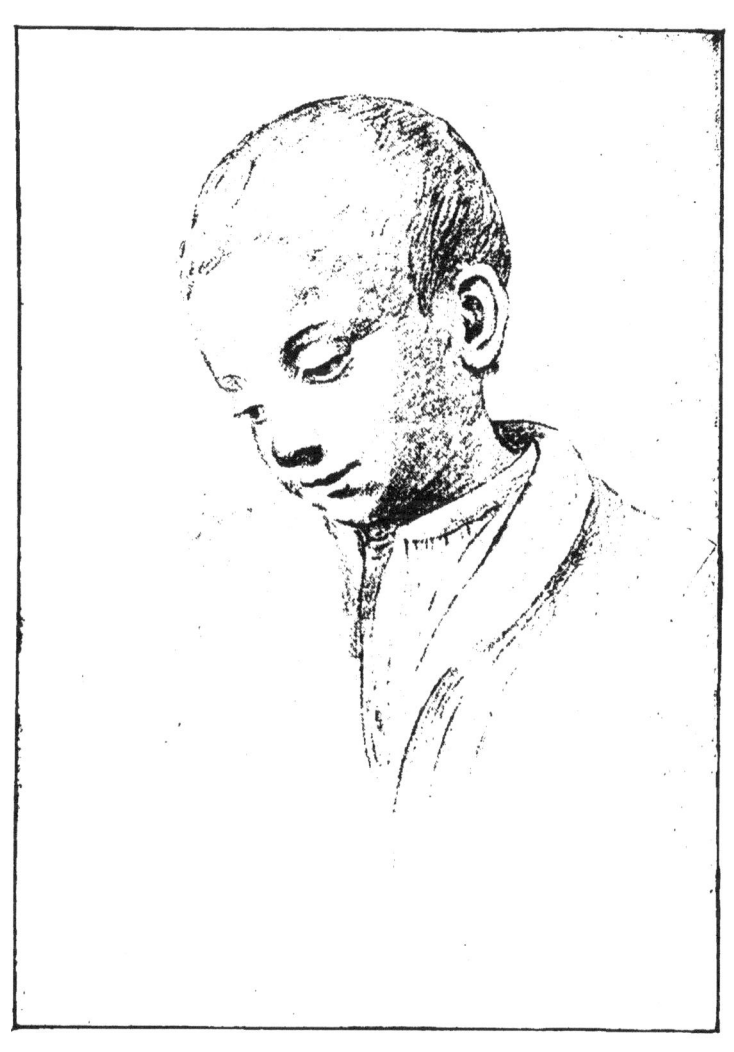

STUDY OF A BOY'S HEAD. *By* FRA BARTOLOMMEO.

men to evil deeds, the people were heated by his
words, and at the Carnival, when it was the custom
to make bonfires on the piazzas, and on the Tuesday
evening to dance round them, Fra Girolamo prevailed
so that they brought to that place pictures and
sculpture, many from the hands of great masters,
and also books, lutes, and songs, and there was great
destruction, especially of pictures. Baccio brought
all the studies and drawings that he had made from
nude figures, and Lorenzo di Credi imitated his
example, and many others also known as Piagnoni.
Also from the affection he bore to Fra Girolamo he
painted his portrait, which was a most beautiful work.
Afterwards it happened that the contrary party rose
against Fra Girolamo to seize him and deliver him
into the hands of justice. The friends of the friar
being aware of it, assembled in S. Mark's to the
number of more than five hundred, and shut themselves up there, Baccio being one of them. But
being indeed a man of little courage, or rather, very
timid and cowardly, when he heard them attack the
convent, and saw some wounded and killed, he began
to be in great fear, and made a vow that if he
escaped he would assume the religious habit. So
when the tumult was over, and the friar was taken
and condemned to death, as historians have related,
Baccio went away to Prato, and made himself a friar
of S. Domenic at that place, as you will find written
in the chronicles of the convent, on the 26th day of

July, 1500, to the great grief of all his friends, who lamented his loss exceedingly, and chiefly because they had heard that he had made up his mind not to have anything more to do with painting.

Mariotto, losing his companion, was almost beside himself, and so strange did it seem to him that he could take no pleasure in anything; and if he had not always disliked the society of friars, whom he constantly spoke against, being of the party that was contrary to the faction of Fra Girolamo, his love for Baccio would have operated so strongly that he would himself have assumed the cowl in the same convent. But Gerozzo Dini prayed him to finish a picture of the Judgment which Baccio had left un-finished, and Fra Bartolommeo entreated him also, having received money for the picture, and his con-science therefore reproaching him; so Mariotto applied himself to it, and completed it with such diligence and earnestness that many would think it was done by one hand alone.

Afterwards Mariotto, with his pupils, painted a picture of the Crucifixion in the Certosa of Florence. But the friars not treating them in the matter of food to their taste, some of the boys who were studying with him, without Mariotto knowing anything about it, contrived to counterfeit the keys of the windows through which the friars received their pittance into their cells, and secretly, sometimes from one and sometimes from another, they stole the food. There

were great complaints on the subject among the
friars, for in questions of eating they are as quick to
feel as others; but the boys doing it dexterously,
and being supposed honest, the blame was laid on
some of the friars, until at last one day the thing was
found out.   Then the friars, that the work might be
finished, consented to give double rations to Mariotto
and his scholars.

Mariotto was a restless person and fond of good
living, and taking a dislike to the mental exertion
necessary to painting, being also often stung by the
tongues of other painters, as is their way, he resolved
to give himself to a less laborious and more jovial
profession, and opened a hostelry outside the gate
S. Gallo, and the tavern of the Dragon at the old
bridge.   This life he led for many months, saying
that he had taken up an art that was without
muscles, foreshortening, or perspective, and what
was better still, without fault-finding, and that the
art that he had given up imitated flesh and blood,
but this made flesh and blood; in this if you had
good wine you heard yourself praised, but in that
every day you were blamed.   But at last the low
life became an annoyance to him, and, filled with
remorse, he returned to painting.

After Fra Bartolommeo had been many months at
Prato, he was sent by his superiors to S. Mark's at
Florence, where the brethren received him gladly.
And in those days Bernardo del Bianco had made a

chapel in the abbey of Florence, and desiring to put a picture there worthy of the ornament, it came into his mind that Fra Bartolommeo would be the right man, and he set all his friends to work to obtain him. Now Fra Bartolommeo was in the convent, thinking of nothing but the holy services and his rule, although the prior had prayed him earnestly, and the friends most dear to him besought him, to paint something, and already four years had passed since he had done anything; but now being pressed by Bernardo del Bianco, he at last began the picture of the Vision of S. Bernard.

Raffaello da Urbino came at this time to study art at Florence, and taught the rules of perspective to Fra Bartolommeo; for Raffaello, being desirous to colour in the friar's manner, was always with him. Afterwards when he heard of the great things that the graceful Raffaello and Michael Angelo were doing in Rome, Fra Bartolommeo obtained leave to go there, and being entertained by Fra Mariano del Piombo, he painted for him two pictures of S. Peter and S. Paul. But because he could not succeed there as he had done at Florence, being, as it were, overwhelmed by the ancient and modern works which he saw in such abundance, he determined to depart, leaving Raffaello to finish one of the pictures, the S. Peter, which was given to Fra Mariano, entirely retouched by Raffaello's hand. So he came back to Florence; and many having reproached him with not being able to paint the human body, he set himself to work to show he was as apt at it as any one else, and painted a S. Sebastian, which received great praise from artists. But the friars removed it from the church, and it was afterwards sent to the king of France.

Fra Bartolommeo held that it was best when you were working to have the things before you, and for the draperies and armour, and such things, he made a model of wood as large as life, with joints, and clothed it with garments, by which he accomplished great things, being able at his pleasure to keep them without being moved until he had finished his work.

While he was painting for Pietro Soderini, in the Council Hall, it happened that he had to work under a window, and the light striking upon him constantly, he was paralyzed on that side, and could not move himself. He was advised, therefore, to go to the baths of S. Filippo, where he stayed a long time, but with little good. Fra Bartolommeo was very fond of fruit, but it was hurtful to him ; and one morning, having eaten a great many figs, he was taken with a violent fever, which cut short his life in four days, at the age of forty-eight. His friends, and especially the friars, mourned him much, and they gave him honourable burial in S. Mark's.

CHAPTER XIII.

THE BELLINI AND ANDREA MANTEGNA.

JACOPO BELLINI, the Venetian painter, had been a pupil of Gentile da Fabriano, and after the departure of Domenico Veniziano from Venice, found himself without a rival there. He had also two sons of fine genius, the one named Giovanni and the other Gentile, named after Gentile da Fabriano, whom he held in memory as his loving master and father. As his two sons grew up, Jacopo himself taught them diligently the principles of drawing, but before long they both surpassed their father greatly. This rejoiced him much, and he constantly encouraged them, saying that as the Tuscans boasted that they grew strong by conquering each other, so he desired that Giovanni should conquer him, and then that he and Gentile should contend together.

He painted many pictures with the aid of his sons on canvas, as they almost always do in that city, using very seldom the panels of maple or poplar, which are so pleasant to paint upon. For if they use wood in Venice, it is always the wood of the fir-tree, which is brought in abundance to that city down the river Adige from Germany. But usually they paint on canvas, either because it does not crack or because you can make the picture any size you will, or for the convenience of sending them about.

Afterwards separating they lived apart, but none the less did the two sons reverence each other, and both their father, praising each the other, and each esteeming himself inferior, thus seeking to surpass one another no less in kindness and courtesy than in the excellence of their art.

The admiration excited by their paintings caused many of the Venetian gentlemen to propose that they should take advantage of the presence of such rare masters to have the Hall of the Great Council painted with stories of the great deeds done by the city in war, and other things worthy of memory. And this work was entrusted by those in rule to Giovanni and Gentile, with Vivarino; but poor Vivarino, having accomplished part with great honour, died, and it was necessary that Giovanni Bellini should complete his work.

Not long after, some portraits having been taken to Turkey to the Grand Turk by an ambassador, that emperor was so struck with astonishment that, although the Mahometan laws prohibit pictures, he accepted them with great goodwill, praising the work without end, and what is more, requesting that

the master himself be sent to him.   But the senate,
considering that Giovanni could ill support the hard·
ships, resolved to send Gentile his brother, and he
was conveyed safely in their galleys to Constantinople, where being presented to Mahomet, he was
received with much kindness as a new thing.   He
presented a beautiful picture to the prince, who
admired it much, and could not persuade himself to
believe that a mortal man had in him so much of
the divinity as to be able to express the things of
nature in such a lively manner.   Gentile painted the
Emperor Mahomet himself from life so well that it
was considered a miracle, and the emperor, having
seen many specimens of his art, asked Gentile if he
had the courage to paint himself, and Gentile having
answered " Yes," before many days were over he
finished a life-like portrait by means of a mirror,
and brought it to the monarch, whose astonishment
was so great that he would have it a divine spirit
dwelt in him.   And had not this art been forbidden
by the law of the Turks, the emperor would never
have let him go.   But either from fear that people
would murmur, or from some other cause, he sent
for him one day, and having thanked him, and given
him great praise, he told him to ask what he would
and it should be granted him without fail.   Gentile
modestly asked for nothing, but that he would graciously give him a letter of recommendation to the
Senate and Signory of Venice.   His request was

granted in as fervent words as possible, and then, loaded with gifts and honours, and with the dignity of a cavalier, he was sent away. Among the other gifts was a chain of gold of two hundred and fifty crowns weight, worked in the Turkish manner. So, leaving Constantinople, he came safely to Venice, where he was received by his brother Giovanni and the whole city with joy, every one rejoicing in the honours which Mahomet had paid him. When the Doge and Signory saw the letters of the emperor, they ordered that a provision of two hundred crowns a year should be paid him all the rest of his life.

Gentile painted a few works after his return; but at last, being near eighty, he passed away to another life, and was buried honourably by his brother Giovanni. Giovanni, widowed of Gentile, whom he had always loved tenderly, continued to work for some time, and having applied himself to painting portraits from life, it became the custom that whoever attained to any rank or position should have their portraits painted by him, or some other. At last, having attained to the age of ninety, he died and was buried by the side of his brother.

Connected with this family by marriage was Andrea Mantegna, who came of very low birth, and when a boy kept cattle in the country round Mantua; but as he grew up, Jacopo Squarcione, a Paduan painter, took him into his house and, perceiving his talents, made him his adopted son.

Squarcione however, knowing himself to be not the best painter in the world, and desiring that Andrea might learn more than he knew himself, made him study from copies of antique statues and pictures, which he fetched from different places, particularly Tuscany and Rome. By these means Andrea learnt much, and began to produce works of so great promise that Jacopo Bellini, the father of Gentile and Giovanni, and the rival of Squarcione, gave him for a wife one of his daughters. But when Squarcione heard of it, he was so enraged with Andrea that he became his enemy, always finding fault with his pictures publicly, saying it would be better if he did not colour his pictures, but made them the colour of marble, for they had no resemblance to life. These reproaches stung Andrea much, but they were of use to him, for he perceived that they were in great part true, and set himself therefore to study from life. Nevertheless it was always Andrea's opinion that for study good antique figures were better than life, because in them the perfection of nature taken from many persons is united, which is rarely the case in one body.

He painted much for Lodovico Gonzaga, Marquis of Mantua, who esteemed him greatly, representing for him the Triumph of Cæsar, which is the best thing he ever did. He gained so much fame by it that Innocent VIII. hearing of him sent for him to Rome. It is said that the Pope, being much occu-

A COMBAT OF SEA-GODS. By ANDREA MANTEGNA.

pied, did not give money to Mantegna as often as he wanted it, and therefore when he was painting the Virtues he put among them Discretion. And the Pope, going one day to see the work, asked Andrea what it was, and he answered, " She is Discretion." So the Pope answered, " If you would have her well accompanied, put by her side Patience." And the painter saw what the Holy Father· meant, and said no more. But when the work was finished, the Pope sent him away with many rewards and favours.

He delighted, as Pollaiuolo did, in engraving, and among other things engraved his Triumph. He was a man of gentle manners, and will be remembered not only in his country but through all the world, so that he deserved to be celebrated by Ariosto at the beginning of the 33rd canto, when, enumerating the most illustrious painters of his time, he says—

" Lionardo, Andrca Mantegna, Gian Eellino."

CHAPTER XIV.

LIONARDO DA VINCI.

ANDREA DEL VERROCCHIO was in his time a gold-smith, sculptor, wood carver, painter, and musician. For having made a name for himself as a goldsmith he was sent for to Rome, to work in the Pope's chapel, and perceiving the great esteem in which the ancient statues which had been found in Rome were held, he determined to apply himself to sculpture, and, entirely abandoning his goldsmith's trade, he set himself to cast some figures in bronze. These being much praised, he took courage and began to work in marble also. Just at that time the wife of Francesco Tornabuoni died, and the husband, who had loved her much, desired to set up a monument to her honour, and entrusted it to Andrea, who carved upon it the death of the lady and three figures of Virtues, which brought him much praise. So he returned to Florence with money, fame, and honour, and was employed to cast in bronze the ornaments for the tomb of Giovanni and Piero di Cosimo de'

Medici, and other works. But finding that he could not increase his fame in this art, being also a person to whom it was not enough to excel in one thing only, he turned his thoughts to painting, and made some sketches for pictures. He began to work upon them in colour, but from some cause they were left unfinished. There are many drawings by his hand, and among them some heads of women, with the hair arranged in that manner that Lionardo da Vinci always imitated.

. The cupola of S. Maria del Fiore was now finished, and after much consultation it was resolved to make the ball of copper, to be placed on the top according to the directions left by Filippo Brunellesco. The work was entrusted to Andrea, and he made it four braccia high, and set it up, fixing it firmly so that the cross could be put upon it securely. The work was finished and set up with great feasting and rejoicing. It required great ingenuity and care, for it had to be made so that it could be entered from below, and strengthened with supports, lest the wind should do it injury.

Andrea was never at rest, but always working at something, though he often changed from one work to another, growing weary of the same thing. Though he never carried out the sketches for pictures which we mentioned before, he did paint some pictures, and among them was one for the friars of Vallombrosa, of S. John baptizing Christ, in which

Lionardo helped him, and which was the cause that
Andrea resolved never to touch a brush again.

At this time the Venetians were desiring to give
honour to Bartolommeo Colleoni da Bergamo, who
had won them many victories; and having heard of
the fame of Andrea, they fetched him to Venice, and
gave him command to make a bronze statue of the
captain, to be set up on the Piazza of S. Giovanni
and S. Paolo. He made therefore the model of a
horse, and was preparing to cast it in bronze, when
it was decided, at the wish of some of the nobles,
that Vellano da Padova should make the figure of
the general, and Andrea the horse only. As soon
as Andrea heard this, he broke off the head and the
legs of his model, and, without saying a word,
returned to Florence in a rage. When the Signory
heard of his departure, they sent a message to him
that he had better not dare ever to return to Venice,
or they would cut off his head, to which he replied
in writing that he *would* take care, for if they cut off
people's heads, it was not in their power to put them
on again, while he could restore the head to the
horse that he had broken off, or a finer one still.
The reply did not displease the Signory, and they
made him return to Venice, doubling the money for
his provision. So he mended his first model, and
cast it in bronze; but he did not perfectly finish it,
for being heated in casting it, he caught a chill, of
which he died in a few days.

Among his many disciples the one he loved most was Lorenzo di Credi. He was the son of Andrea Sciarpelloni, and was apprenticed by his father to Master Credi the goldsmith, where before long he became so excellent in the work to the great honour of Credi that he was always called not Lorenzo Sciarpelloni, but Lorenzo di Credi. Afterwards he attached himself to Andrea Verrocchio, having Piero Perugino and Lionardo da Vinci for his companions; and because Lionardo's manner of painting pleased him greatly, he learnt to imitate him. Lorenzo was so much beloved by his master that when Andrea went to Venice he left Lorenzo in charge of all his business and his revenues, with all his drawings and statues and materials for work. And Lorenzo on his side was so attached to his master that, besides attending to his affairs in Florence with wonderful affection, he went more than once to Venice to see him and render him account of his management. This gave Andrea so much satisfaction that, if Lorenzo would have consented, he would have made him his heir. When Andrea died Lorenzo went to Venice and brought his body back to Florence, giving up to the heirs everything that was Andrea's, except the statues and drawings and things of art.

But the greatest of all his pupils was Lionardo da Vinci, in whom, besides a beauty of person never sufficiently admired and a wonderful grace in all his actions, there was such a power of intellect that whatever he turned his mind to he made himself master of with ease.

Marvellous and divine, indeed, was Lionardo the son of Ser Piero da Vinci. In erudition and letters he would have distinguished himself, if he had not been variable and unstable. For he set himself to learn many things, and when he had begun them gave them up. In arithmetic during the few months that he applied himself to it, he made such progress that he often perplexed his master by the doubts and difficulties that he propounded. He gave some time to the study of music, and learnt to play on the lute, improvising songs most divinely. But though he applied himself to such various subjects, he never laid aside drawing and modelling in relief, to which his fancy inclined him more than to anything else ; which Ser Piero perceiving, he took some of his drawings one day and carried them to Andrea del Verrocchio, with whom he was in close friendship, and prayed him to say whether he thought, if Lionardo gave himself up to drawing, he would succeed. Andrea was astounded at the great beginning Lionardo had made, and urged Ser Piero to make him apply himself to it. So he arranged with Lionardo that he was to go to Andrea's workshop, which Lionardo did very willingly, and set himself to practise every art in which design has a part. For he had such a marvellous mind that, being a good geometrician, he not only worked at modelling (making while a boy.

A WARRIOR. By LIONARDO DA VINCI.

.

some laughing women's heads, and some heads of children which seem to have come from a master's hand), but also made many designs for architecture ; and he was the first, while he was still quite young, to discuss the question of making a channel for the river Arno from Pisa to Florence. He made models of mills and presses, and machines to be worked by water, and designs for tunnelling through mountains, or levers and cranes for raising great weights, so that it seemed that his brain never ceased inventing ; and many of these drawings are still scattered about. Among them was one drawn for some of the citizens then governing Florence, to show how it would be possible to lift up the church of S. Giovanni, and put steps under it without throwing it down ; and he supported his scheme with such strong reasons as made it appear possible, though as soon as he was gone every one felt in his mind how impossible it really was.

He delighted much in horses and also in all other animals, and often when passing by the places where they sold birds he would take them out of their cages, and paying the price that was asked for them, would let them fly away into the air, restoring to them their lost liberty.

While, as we have said, he was studying art under Andrea del Verrocchio, the latter was painting a picture of S. John baptizing Christ ; Lionardo worked upon an angel who was holding the clothes, and

although he was so young, he managed it so well
that Lionardo's angel was better than Andrea's
figures, which was the cause of Andrea's never touching colours again, being angry that a boy should
know more than he.

There is a story that Ser Piero, being at his country
house, was asked by one of the country people to get
a round piece of wood, which he had cut from a fig-
tree, painted for him in Florence, which he very
willingly undertook to do, as the man was skilled in
catching birds and fishing, and was very serviceable
to Ser Piero in these sports. So having it brought
to Florence without telling Lionardo where it came
from, he asked him to paint something upon it.
Lionardo, finding it crooked and rough, straightened
it by means of fire, and gave it to a turner that it
might be made smooth and even.   Then having
prepared it for painting, he began to think what he
could paint upon it that would frighten every one
that saw it, having the effect of the head of Medusa.
So he brought for this purpose to his room, which
no one entered but himself, lizards, grasshoppers,
serpents, butterflies, locusts, bats, and other strange
animals of the kind, and from them all he produced
a great animal so horrible and fearful that it seemed
to poison the air with its fiery breath. This he represented coming out of some dark broken rocks,
with venom issuing from its open jaws, fire from its
eyes, and smoke from its nostrils, a monstrous and

horrible thing indeed. And he suffered much in
doing it, for the smell in the room of these dead
animals was very bad, though Lionardo did not feel
it from the love he bore to art. When the work was
finished, Lionardo told his father that he could send
for it when he liked. And Ser Piero going one
morning to the room for it, when he knocked at the
door, Lionardo opened it, and telling him to wait a
little, turned back into the room, placed the picture
in the light, and arranged the window so as to
darken the room a little, and then brought him in to
see it. Ser Piero at the first sight started back, not
perceiving that the figure that he saw was painted,
and was turning to go, when Lionardo stopped him
saying, " The work answers the purpose for which
it was made. Take it then, for that was the effect I
wanted to produce." The thing seemed marvellous
to Ser Piero and he praised greatly Lionardo's
whimsical idea. And secretly buying from a merchant another circular piece of wood, painted with a
heart pierced with a dart, he gave it to the countryman, who remained grateful to him as long as he
lived. But Lionardo's Ser Piero sold to some merchants in Florence for a hundred ducats, and it
soon came into the hands of the Duke of Milan, who
bought it of them for three hundred ducats.

Lionardo was so pleased whenever he saw a
strange head or beard or hair of unusual appearance that he would follow such a person a whole

day, and so learn him by heart, that when he
reached home he could draw him as if he were
present. There are many of these heads to be
seen, both of men and women, such as the head
of Americo Vespucci, which is the head of an old
man most beautifully drawn in chalk; and also
of Scaramuccia, captain of the gypsies. When
Giovan Galeazzo, Duke of Milan, was dead, and
Lodovico Sforza became duke in the year 1494,
Lionardo was brought to Milan to play the lute
before him, in which he greatly delighted. Lionardo
brought an instrument which he had made himself,
a new and strange thing made mostly of silver, in
the form of a horse's head, that the tube might be
larger and the sound more sonorous, by which he
surpassed all the other musicians who were assembled
there. Besides, he was the best improvisatore of
his time. The duke, hearing his marvellous discourse, became enamoured of his talents to an incredible degree, and prayed him to paint an altar-
piece of the Nativity, which he sent to the emperor.

He also painted in Milan for the friars of S.
Domenic, at S. Maria delle Grazie, a Last Supper,
a thing most beautiful and marvellous. He gave to
the heads of the apostles great majesty and beauty,
but left that of Christ imperfect, not thinking it
possible to give that celestial divinity which is
required for the representation of Christ. The work
finished after this sort has always been held by the

Milanese in the greatest veneration, and by strangers also, because Lionardo imagined, and has succeeded in expressing, the desire that has entered the minds of the apostles to know who is betraying their Master. So in the face of each one may be seen love, fear, indignation, or grief at not being able to understand the meaning of Christ; and this excites no less astonishment than the obstinate hatred and treachery to be seen in Judas. Besides this, every lesser part of the work shows an incredible diligence; even in the table-cloth the weaver's work is imitated in a way that could not be better in the thing itself.

It is said that the prior of the place was very importunate in urging Lionardo to finish the work, it seeming strange to him to see Lionardo standing half a day lost in thought; and he would have liked him never to have put down his pencil, as if it were a work like digging the garden. And this not being enough, he complained to the duke, and was so hot about it that he was constrained to send for Lionardo and urge him to the work. Lionardo, knowing the prince to be acute and intelligent, was ready to discuss the matter with him, which he would not do with the prior. He reasoned about art, and showed him that men of genius may be working when they seem to be doing the least, working out inventions in their minds and forming those perfect ideas which afterwards they express with their hands. He added that he still had two heads to do; that of Christ, which he would not seek for in the world, and which he could not hope that his imagination would be able to conceive of such beauty and celestial grace as was fit for the incarnate divinity. Besides this, that of Judas was wanting, which he was considering, not thinking himself capable of imagining a form to express the face of him who after receiving so many benefits had a soul so evil that he was resolved to betray his Lord and the creator of the world; but this second he was looking for, and if he could find no better there was always the head of this importunate and foolish prior. This moved the duke marvellously to laughter, and he said he was a thousand times right. So the poor prior, quite confused, left off urging him and left him alone, and Lionardo finished Judas's head, which is a true portrait of treachery and cruelty. But that of Christ, as we have said, he left imperfect. The excellence of this picture, both in composition and incomparable finish of execution, made the King of France desire to carry it into his kingdom, and he tried every way to find architects who could bring it safely, not considering the expense, so much he desired to have it. But as it was painted on the wall his Majesty could not have his will, and it remained with the Milanese.

In the refectory, and while he was working at the Last Supper, he painted Lodovico with his eldest son, Massimiliano, and on the other side the Duchess

Beatrice with Francesco her other son, both afterwards Dukes of Milan. While he was employed upon
this work he proposed to the duke that he should
make a bronze equestrian statue of marvellous size
to perpetuate the memory of the Duke (Francesco
Sforza). He began it, but made the model of such
a size that it could never be completed. There are
some who say that Lionardo began it so large
because he did not mean to finish it, as with
many of his other things. But in truth his mind,
being so surpassingly great, was often brought to
a stand because it was too venturesome, and the
cause of his leaving so many things imperfect
was his search for excellence after excellence, and
perfection after perfection. And those who saw
the clay model that Lionardo made, said they had
never seen anything more beautiful or more superb,
and this was in existence until the French came to
Milan with Louis king of France, when they broke
it to pieces. There was also a small model in wax,
which is lost, which was considered perfect, and a
book of the anatomy of the horse which he made in
his studies. Afterwards with greater care he gave
himself to the study of human anatomy, aided by,
and in his turn aiding, that Messer Marc Antonio
della Torre who was one of the first to shed light
upon anatomy, which up to that time had been lost
in the shades of ignorance. In this he was much
helped by Lionardo, who made a book with drawings

in red chalk, outlined with a pen, of the bones and
muscles which he had dissected with his own hand.
There are also some writings of Lionardo written
backward with the left hand, treating of painting
and methods of drawing and colouring.

In his time the King of France came to Milan,
and Lionardo was entreated to make something
strange for his reception, upon which he constructed
a lion, which advanced some steps and then opened
his breast and showed it full of lilies. Having
returned to Florence, he found that the Servite
monks had intrusted Filippino with the work of
painting an altar-piece; but when Filippino heard
that Lionardo had said he should have liked such a
piece of work, like the courteous man he was, he
left off working at it, and the friars brought Lionardo
to their convent that he might paint it, providing
both for himself and his household. For a long
time, however, he did nothing, but at last he made a
cartoon of our Lady with S. Anne and the infant
Christ, which not only astonished all artists, but
when it was finished, for two days his room was
filled with men and women, young and old, going as
to a solemn festival to see Lionardo's marvels. This
cartoon afterwards went to France. But he gave up
the work for the friars, who recalled Filippino, but
he was surprised by death before he could finish it.

Lionardo undertook to paint for Francesco del
Giocondo a portrait of Mona Lisa his wife, but

having spent four years upon it, left it unfinished.
This work now belongs to King Francis of France,
and whoever wishes to see how art can imitate
nature may learn from this head. Mona Lisa
being most beautiful, he used, while he was painting
her, to have men to sing and play to her and buffoons
to amuse her, to take away that look of melancholy
which is so often seen in portraits; and in this of
Lionardo's there is a peaceful smile more divine
than human. By the excellence of the works of
this most divine of artists his fame was grown so
great that all who delighted in art, and in fact the
whole city, desired to have some memorial of it.
And the Gonfalonier and the chief citizens agreed
that the Great Hall of the Council, having been
rebuilt, Lionardo should be charged to paint some
great work there. Therefore, accepting the work,
Lionardo began a cartoon representing the story of
Niccolò Piccinino, captain of the Duke Filippo of
Milan, in which he drew a group of cavalry fighting
for a standard, representing vividly the rage and
fury both of the men and the horses, two of which,
with their fore feet entangled, are making war no less
fiercely with their teeth than those who ride them.
We cannot describe the variety of the soldiers' garments, with their crests and other ornaments, and
the masterly power he showed in the forms of the
horses, whose muscular strength and beauty of grace
he knew better than any other man. It is said that

for drawing this cartoon he erected an ingenious scaffolding that could be raised and lowered. And desiring to paint the wall in oil, he made a composition to cover the wall, but when he began to paint upon it, it proved so unsuccessful that he shortly abandoned it altogether.

There is a story that having gone to the bank for the sum which he was accustomed to receive from the Gonfalonier Piero Soderini every month, the cashier wanted to give him some packets of farthings, but he refused to take them, saying, " I am no farthing painter." As some accused him of having cheated Soderini in not finishing the picture, there arose murmurs against him, upon which Lionardo, by the help of his friends, collected the money and restored it to him, but Piero would not accept it.

When Leo was made Pope, Lionardo went to Rome with Duke Giuliano de' Medici, and knowing the Pope to be fond of philosophy, especially alchemy, he used to make little animals of a wax paste, which as he walked along he would fill with wind by blowing into them, and so make them fly in the air, until the wind being exhausted they dropped to the ground. The vinedresser of the Belvedere having found a very strange lizard, Lionardo made some wings of the scales of other lizards and fastened them on its back with a mixture of quicksilver, so that they trembled when it walked; and having made for it eyes, horns, and a beard, he tamed it and kept it in a box, but all his friends to whom he showed it used to run away from fear.

It is said that when the Pope entrusted him with some work for him he immediately began to distil oil for the varnish, upon which Pope Leo said, "Oh, this is a man to do nothing, for he thinks of the end before he begins his work."

There was great ill-feeling between him and Michael Angelo Buonarroti, on which account Michael Angelo left Florence. But when Lionardo heard this, he set out and went into France, where the king, having already some of his works, was well affectioned towards him, and desired that he should colour his cartoon of S. Anne; but he, according to his custom, kept him waiting a long time. At last, having become old, he lay ill for many months, and seeing himself near death, he set himself to study the holy Christian religion, and though he could not stand, desired to leave his bed with the help of his friends and servants to receive the Holy Sacrament. Then the king, who used often and lovingly to visit him, came in, and he, raising himself respectfully to sit up in bed, spoke of his sickness, and how he had offended God and man by not working at his art as he ought. Then there came on a paroxysm, a forerunner of death, and the king raised him and lifted his head to help him and lessen the pain, whereupon his spirit, knowing it could have no greater honour, passed away in the king's arms in the seventh-fifth year of his age.

. The loss of Lionardo was mourned out of measure by all who had known him, for there was none who had done such honour to painting. The splendour of his great beauty could calm the saddest soul, and his words could move the most obstinate mind. His great strength could restrain the most violent fury, and he could bend an iron knocker or a horseshoe as if it were lead. He was liberal to his friends, rich and poor, if they had talent and worth; and indeed as Florence had the greatest of gifts in his birth, so she suffered an infinite loss in his death.

I think I have said that it was in the little town of Vinci in the Valdarno that Ser Piero the father of the great Lionardo dwelt. To this Piero was born after Lionardo another son, Bartolommeo, who remained at Vinci, and when he was come to years of discretion, took to wife one of the first ladies of the town. Bartolommeo was very desirous of having a son, and he used often to tell his wife of the great genius of his brother Lionardo, and to pray God to make her worthy to bring forth another Lionardo, he being already dead. And when according to his desire a boy was born, he desired to name it Lionardo, but by the counsel of his relations he gave it the name of Piero after his father. At the age of three years it was a child of beautiful countenance and curling hair, with much grace in all its gestures and a wonderful quickness of mind. And there came to Vinci and lodged in the house of Bartolommeo an excellent astrologer named Giuliano del Carmine, and with him a priest skilled in palmistry, and they, looking at the head and hand of the child, predicted both of them alike that he would be a great genius, and in a very short time would make great progress in the arts, but that his life would be very short. And too true was their prophecy!

Piero, then, as he grew was taught his letters by his father, but without a master he set himself to draw and to make little figures of clay, so Bartolommeo trusted that his prayer had been heard and his brother given back to him in his son. Therefore, taking him to Florence, he placed him first with Bandinello and afterwards with Il Tribolo. This master being then employed on some fountains at Castello, set Piero to work upon the figure of a boy, and he finished this so well that Il Tribolo prophesied he would show himself of rare skill. Taking courage by his success, he produced other works which astonished those who saw them. At this time few knew that he was the nephew of Lionardo da Vinci, but when his works had made him known, it was discovered of what family he came, and they left off calling him Piero and called him Il Vinci. Il Vinci therefore, having heard much of Rome, felt a great desire to go there, not only to see the antiquities, but also Michael Angelo's works and himself, then living in Rome. He went therefore with some of his friends, but having seen all that he desired, returned to Florence, considering wisely that the works there were too profound for him, and should be seen not by beginners, but by those who have greater knowledge of art. Nevertheless after more study he returned again to Rome, and spent there a year making many things worthy of memory, and for his friend Luca Martini he made a copy in wax of Michael Angelo's Moses. While he was there Luca Martini was made by the Duke of Florence Proveditore of Pisa. And not forgetting his friend, he wrote to him that he had prepared a room for him and provided a piece of marble. Vinci therefore, moved by this invitation and the love he bore to Luca, left Rome and chose Pisa for his residence for some time. And the duke being then intent on benefiting and embellishing the city of Pisa, Il Vinci was employed by him.

Il Vinci's name and talents were now known and admired by all, and being still young, it appeared likely that he would equal any man in art, when the term prescribed by Heaven came to an end, and his rapid course was stopped. It happened that the duke sent Luca Martini to Genoa on matters of importance, and he loving Il Vinci and his company, and thinking it would be an amusement to him to see Genoa, took him with him. But almost immediately he was seized with a fever, and the distress was doubled by his friend being obliged to leave him and return to the Duke in Florence. He commended him to the care of Abate Nero; but Il Vinci, finding himself growing daily worse, sent for one of his pupils from Pisa, and with his aid was brought to Leghorn by water, and thence to Pisa in a litter. Arriving at Pisa one evening at twenty-two o'clock, worn out with the hardships of the road and the sea and the fever, he could get no rest that night, and the next morning at break of day passed away to another life, not having reached the age of three and twenty.

CHAPTER XV.

At the same time that Florence was acquiring such fame by the works of Lionardo, Venice received no little honour by the talents and excellence of one of its citizens, who far surpassed the Bellini, whom they held in such esteem, and every other who had up to that time painted in their city. This was Giorgio, born at Castelfranco in the Trevisan in the year 1478, and from his fine person and the greatness of his soul, afterwards called Giorgione, who though of low birth was all his life distinguished for his gentle manners. He was brought up in Venice, and sang and played so divinely that he was often invited to musical entertainments, and received by noble persons. He gave himself, however, to drawing, and nature favoured him so much that he, falling in love with her beauties, would never use anything in his works which he had not drawn from life; so that he acquired the name not only of having surpassed Gentile and Giovanni Bellini, but of having equalled those who worked in Tuscany, and were the authors of the modern manner. Giorgione had seen some things of Lionardo's with great depth of shadow but blended and softened, and this manner pleased him so much that all his life he used it and imitated it when painting in oil.

It was in 1504 that a great fire destroyed the German Exchange near the bridge of the Rialto, consuming all the merchandize, to the very great loss of the merchants. The Signory of Venice ordered that it should be rebuilt, and it was speedily completed, with greater accommodation and magnificence and beauty; and the fame of Giorgione having by this time grown great, it was decided by those in authority that he should paint it in fresco according to his own fancy, provided he displayed his utmost powers, and made an excellent work of it, for it was in the best situation, and the finest view of the whole city. Giorgione, setting to work, thought only how he could design figures that would best display his art; and in fact there is no story in it, nor does it represent the story of any person, ancient or modern. I for my part have never understood it, nor have I ever found anybody who did; for here is a woman and there a man, in certain attitudes, one with the head of a lion near him, and the other with an angel in the guise of Cupid. In short, his figures look well together, and there are heads very well drawn and coloured, and all he did was evidently from life, and not in imitation of any manner.

There is a story that Giorgione was talking to some sculptors at the time that Andrea Verrocchio was making his bronze horse, and they contended that because sculpture showed in one figure different sides, and could be seen all round, it surpassed painting, which only showed one part. Giorgione argued that a picture could show all sorts of views of a man at one glance, without his having to walk round it, and he undertook to show in one picture the back and the front and the two sides of one single figure, a thing which puzzled them ; but he did it in this way. He painted a man, turning his back to the spectators, and having at his feet some smooth water, in which the front view was reflected, on one side of him was a polished corslet which he had taken off, on which was plainly reflected his left profile, while on the other hand was a mirror, in which might be clearly seen his other side—a fanciful conceit which was highly admired.

He made many portraits of different Italian princes, and painted from life Caterina, Queen of Cyprus. But while he was expecting still to add to his honours and those of his country, he fell ill of the plague, in the year 1511, and at the age of thirty-four passed to another life, to the infinite grief of his many friends and with damage to the world who lost him.. Nevertheless there remained his two excellent pupils, Sebastiano Veniziano del Piombo and Titian, who not only equalled him but greatly

surpassed him. Sebastiano's first profession was
not painting but music, which made him very ac-
ceptable to the nobles of Venice, with whom he lived
on intimate terms. But when still young, desiring
to learn painting, he studied first with Giovanni
Bellini, who was then an old man. Afterwards,
when Giorgione had introduced a more modern
manner, Sebastiano left Bellini and joined Giorgione,
and stayed with him until he had acquired his style
so accurately that many who have no great knowledge of art mistake his works for Giorgione's.

A rich merchant of Sienna, Agostino Chigi, hearing
of his fame, sought to persuade him to go to Rome,
being pleased not only with his painting but also with
his music and his agreeable conversation. It was
not hard to persuade Bastiano to go, for he knew
that that city had always been the protector of men
of genius. So when he was come to Rome Agostino
set him to work, and he did some things in Agostino's
palace in the style that he had brought from Venice,
very different from that which the best painters in
Rome employed. Afterwards Raffaello, having
painted the story of Galatea in the same place,
Bastiano painted by the side of it a Polyphemus.
He also painted some things in oil, and having learnt
a soft style of colouring from Giorgione, he obtained
by them a great reputation.

Raffaello by this time had earned such honour by
his paintings that his friends and adherents said that

they were better than Michael Angelo's, being pleasant
in colouring, fine in invention, excellent in expression,
and good in drawing, while Buonarroti's had none of
these qualities but the drawing.   And so they said
that Raffaello was at least equal to him in drawing,
and surpassed him in his colour.   But Sebastiano
was not of these, being a man of exquisite judgment.
So Michael Angelo being drawn towards Sebastiano,
and being pleased with his colouring and graceful
style, took him under his protection, thinking that,
if he aided Sebastiano in his drawing, he could
through him contend with those who opposed him.
Sebastiano's paintings being therefore more highly
valued through the praise that Michael Angelo had
given them, a gentleman from Viterbo much favoured
by the Pope gave Sebastiano a picture of a dead
Christ to paint for a chapel in San Francesco at
Viterbo.   But though Sebastiano carried it out with
great diligence, the design was by Michael Angelo.
The work was held by all who saw it to be most
beautiful, and Sebastiano gained great credit by it.
And Pier Francesco Borgherini, a Florentine merchant, having taken a chapel in S. Piero in Montorio,
entrusted the painting of it to Sebastiano, thinking,
as was indeed the case, that Michael Angelo would
make the design.   Sebastiano carried it out with
great diligence and care, and thinking he had found
a way of painting in oil on a wall, he covered the
plaster with a suitable preparation, and all that part

which has the scourging of Christ he painted in oil.
Nor will I conceal that many think that Michael
Angelo not only made a little drawing for the work,
but that the figure of Christ was put in altogether
by him, there being a great difference between that
and the other figures. When Sebastiano had uncovered this work his enemies' tongues were silenced,
and few ventured to attack him. Afterwards, when
Raffaello painted for the Cardinal de' Medici that
picture of the Transfiguration which was placed
after his death in S. Piero in Montorio, Sebastiano
painted another picture of the same size, as if in
rivalry, representing the raising of Lazarus, and this
also was worked under the guidance of Michael
Angelo, and in some parts from his drawings. The
two pictures when they were finished were exhibited
together, and both received great praise, for although
Raffaello's works have no equals for grace and beauty,
yet none the less Sebastiano's efforts were universally
applauded.

This man had to labour greatly at all his works;
they did not come with the facility that nature and
study sometimes give. So in the chapel of Agostino
Chigi, where Raffaello had made the sibyls and
prophets, there was a niche below in which Bastiano
undertook to paint something to surpass Raffaello,
and set to work to prepare the wall; but he left it
untouched when he died ten years after. Sebastiano
indeed could draw quickly and easily from life, but

it was just the contrary in subject pictures. Indeed
portrait painting was his true work.

When Cardinal Giulio de' Medici was made Pope
under the name of Clement VII., he intimated to
Sebastiano that he would seek occasion to favour
him. Therefore, upon the death of Fra Mariano
Fetti, the Frate del Piombo, Sebastiano reminded
him of his promise, and made request for the office
of the Piombo. And although Giovanni da Udine,
who had served his Holiness long, preferred the
same request, the Pope gave orders that Sebastiano
should have the office, on the agreement to pay to
Giovanni a pension of three hundred crowns. So
Sebastiano assumed the habit of a friar, and at the
same time his nature seemed to change; for having
wherewith to satisfy his desires without using his
pencil, he let it repose, and made up for his laborious
days by rest and ease. Thus the magnificent
liberality of Clement VII. rewarding Sebastiano too
highly was the cause that from a hardworking,
industrious man he became slothful and negligent,
and having laboured constantly when he was competing with Raffaello, and his fortune was low, he did
the contrary as soon as he had enough. He had a
very good house, which he had built himself, and in
this he lived in the greatest contentment, without
any wish to paint. He used to say that it was just
as prudent to live a quiet life as to be ever struggling
restlessly to leave a great name behind. And he

acted according to his words, having always the best wines and rarest dainties he could get, taking more account of good living than of art. Being censured by some, who said it was a shame that now that he had the means of living he worked no more, he answered, "Now that I have the means of living I do no work, because there are clever men in the world now, who can do in two months as much as I used to do in two years, and I think if I live much longer everything will have been painted; so as these men do so much, it is a good thing that there should be some who do nothing, that they may have more to do." And in pleasantries of this kind he would run on, and indeed there was no better companion than he.

As we have said, Bastiano was much beloved by Michael Angelo, but when the Pope's chapel was to be painted, where now is Michael Angelo's Judgment, there was some ill-feeling between them. For Fra Sebastiano had persuaded the Pope to make Michael Angelo paint it in oil, whereas he would not do it except in fresco. Michael Angelo therefore saying neither yes or no, the wall was prepared in Fra Sebastiano's way; Michael Angelo left it untouched for some months, and when they implored him to begin it, he said at last that he would not do it except in fresco, for oil painting was an art for women and lazy people like Fra Sebastiano. So the plaster being taken down it was prepared for working in fresco, and Michael Angelo set to work upon it, but never forgot the injury Fra Sebastiano had done him.

Fra Sebastiano, having brought himself to doing nothing whatever except the work of his office, and living well, fell sick at last of a violent fever and died. Art lost little by his death, for he might have been counted among those whom it had lost from the time he put on the friar's habit; but many of his friends mourn him still for his pleasant converse. He had at different times many young men with him to study art, but to no great profit, for they learnt little from him but how to live well.

CHAPTER XVI.

PERUGINO AND RAFFAELLO.

OF what great use poverty may be to genius, and
how it may be powerful in perfecting it, may be
clearly seen in the life of Pietro Perugino, who,
driven from Perugia by want, came to Florence, desiring to make a position for himself by his talents.
For many months, having no other bed to lie on, he
slept in a box, applying himself with the utmost
fervour to the study of his profession, and knowing
no other pleasure than painting. For he had always
before his eyes the fear of poverty, and he was
spurred by want, desiring, if he could not be highest
and supreme, at least to have wherewith to support
himself. Therefore he cared neither for cold, nor
hunger, nor discomfort, nor fatigue, that he might
one day live at ease, quoting always the proverb,
that after bad weather must come good, and that
in fine weather you should build the house to cover
you when you need it.

According to the common story, he was born in

Perugia, the son of a poor man of Castello della Pieve, named Cristofano, who gave him in baptism the name of Pietro. Growing up in misery and want, he was apprenticed to a painter of Perugia, who, though he was not very good at his trade, held in great veneration art and the men who excelled in it. He did nothing but impress upon Pietro what an honour and advantage painting was to those who practised it well, relating the glory of ancient and modern painters, by which he kindled in Pietro the desire to become one of them. So he used to be always asking where men could prepare themselves for the trade best, and his master always answered in the same way, that it was in Florence more than anywhere else that men grew perfect in all the arts, especially painting. For in that city men are spurred by three things : First there are many there ready to find fault, the air of the place making men independent in mind and not easily contented with mediocre works. Secondly, if a man wished to live there he must be industrious, for Florence, not having a large and fertile country, could not provide for the wants of those who dwelt there at little expense. And thirdly, there is the desire of glory and honour, which the air excites to a high degree in men of every profession, so that no man who has any spirit will consent to be like others, much less be left behind.

Moved therefore by this advice, Pietro came to Florence and studied under the discipline of Andrea

Verrocchio. And in a few years he obtained such
reputation that not only were Florence and Italy
full of his works, but they were sent also to France,
Spain, and many other countries, and the merchants
began to purchase them that they might send them
abroad to their own great profit.

There is a story which I have heard told of a prior
of a convent who had employed him to paint in its
cloisters; and this prior was very good at making
ultramarine. Having therefore abundance of it, he
desired that Pietro should put a great deal into his
works; he was, however, so miserably suspicious
that he would not trust Pietro, but would always be
present when he was using the ultramarine. Pietro,
being by nature upright and honest, took it ill that
the prior should distrust him, and thought how he
could shame him out of it. So he took a basin of
water, and setting himself to his work, for every two
brushfuls that he took he washed his brush in the
basin, so that there was more colour left in the water
than he put into his work. The prior, seeing his bag
getting empty, and the picture not getting on, kept
saying, "Oh, how much ultramarine that plaster
consumes!" "You see!" answered Pietro. But
when the prior was gone, Pietro collected the ultramarine that was at the bottom of the basin; and
when the time seemed to him to be come, he gave it
back to the prior, saying, "Father, this is yours;
learn to trust honest men who never deceive those

who trust in them, but know how to deceive, when they choose, suspicious men like you."

The fame of Pietro was so spread abroad in Italy that he was sent for by Pope Sixtus IV. to work in his chapel in the company of many excellent artists; but these works were destroyed in the time of Pope Paul III. to make place for the Judgment of the divine Michael Angelo. Pietro worked so much, and had always so much to do, that he often put the same things into his pictures, and his art was reduced to a manner, so that he gave to all his figures the same air. About this time, Michael Angelo having appeared, Pietro greatly desired to see his works from the report which artists gave of them. But perceiving that he himself would be eclipsed by the greatness of him who had made so great a beginning, in his anger he attacked with bitter words many of the artists in Florence. Therefore he deserved that not only other artists should attack him, but that also Michael Angelo should say in public that his art was rude. But Pietro could not endure such an insult, and the matter was brought before the magistrates; nevertheless Pietro came off with little honour. When his friends told him that he had wandered away from the good path, either from avarice or from fear of losing time, Pietro answered, "I have put into my work the figures which you formerly praised and which pleased you greatly. If now they displease you, what am I to do? '

Therefore when sonnets were written upon him at-
tacking him, he left Florence and returned to Perugia,
where he painted in fresco in the church of S. Severo,
the young Raffaello da Urbino, his pupil, doing some
of the figures.   He also began a work in fresco of no
little importance at Castello della Pieve, but did not
finish it.   Pietro, as if he could trust nobody, used
to carry about him all the money he had, as he went
backwards and forwards to Castello ; so it fell out
that some men, laying wait for him, robbed him, but
at his earnest entreaty they spared his life.   Afterwards, by means of his friends, he recovered a great
part of the money that had been taken from him ;
nevertheless he was near dying of grief.   For Pietro
was a man of very little religion, and would never
believe in the immortality of the soul.   His hope
was all set on the gifts of fortune, and he would have
done anything for money.   He had a most beautiful
young woman for his wife, and took so much pleasure
in seeing her well adorned, both at home and abroad,
that it is said he often dressed her with his own
hands.

He died at last in Castello della Pieve an old man of
seventy-eight.   He made many masters in painting,
and one who surpassed him by a long way, the wonderful Raffaello Sanzio da Urbino.   Pinturicchio, the
Perugian painter, was also his pupil, who, although he
executed many works, had a much greater name than
he deserved.   He was called to Sienna by Cardinal

Piccolomini to paint the library erected there by
Pope Pius II. But the sketches and drawings for
these pictures were all by the hand of Raffaello, then
very young, who had been his schoolfellow under
Pietro. He worked also in Rome under Pope Sixtus,
and painted an infinite number of pictures all over
Italy, which not being very excellent I will pass
over in silence.

When he was fifty-nine years of age he was charged
to paint the Birth of our Lady in S. Francesco in
Sienna, and the friars there gave him a room to
dwell in, which at his desire they emptied of everything except a great chest, which seemed to them too
big to move. But Pinturicchio, being a strange, fanciful man, made so much disturbance about it that the
friars at last set to work to carry it away, and in
moving it a plank gave way, and discovered five
hundred ducats of gold. Pinturicchio, however, was
so much vexed at the friars' good fortune that, not
being able to forget it, he fell sick and died.

His great schoolfellow, Raffaello, one of those
possessed of such rare gifts that they cannot be
called simply men, but, if it is allowable so to speak,
rather mortal gods, was born in the famous city of
Urbino in Italy, in the year 1483, on Good Friday,
at three o'clock of the night, being the son of Giovanni de' Santi, a not very excellent painter, but a
man of good understanding, and capable of directing
his son in that good way which unfortunately had

not been shown to himself in his youth. And because Giovanni knew of what consequence it was that the child should be nursed by his own mother and not left to the care of a hired nurse, he kept him in his own house that he might learn good ways, rather than the rough customs of common men. And as soon as he was grown, he began to teach him painting, so that it was not long before he was able to help his father in many of his works. But at last the good father, knowing how little his son could learn from him, determined to put him with Pietro Perugino, and going to Perugia, told him his desire. And Pietro, who was very courteous, and a lover of men of talent, accepted Raffaello. Therefore Giovanni, returning joyfully to Urbino, took the boy, not without many tears, from his mother, who tenderly loved him, and brought him to Perugia. And when Pietro saw his manner of drawing and his pleasant ways, he pronounced that judgment upon him which time has proved most true. It is a very remarkable thing that while Raffaello was studying under Pietro he imitated him so closely that it is impossible to distinguish their works.

When Pinturicchio was entrusted with the painting of the library of Sienna, he took Raffaello with him, but while they were there, some painters spoke to him with such great praise of the cartoons of Lionardo da Vinci and Michael Angelo at Florence, that the desire came upon him to see them, and he

set out for Florence ; and arriving there was no less
pleased with the city than with the works he came
to see, and he determined to tarry there some time,
making friends with many young painters.   But
after he had been to Florence he changed his manner
greatly, for while there he studied the old works of
Masaccio and the labours of Lionardo and Michael
Angelo, and he was in close intercourse with Fra
Bartolommeo di S. Marco, whose colour pleasing
him much, he sought to imitate it, while in return
he taught the good father perspective.

Then Bramante da Urbino, who was in the service
of Julius II., being distantly related to Raffaello and
of the same district, wrote to him that he had been
using his influence with the Pope to obtain for him
leave to show his powers in certain rooms of the
palace.   The tidings pleased Raffaello, and leaving
his works at Florence unfinished, he departed for
Rome, where he found that a great part of the
chambers of the palace had been already painted, or
were being painted, by other masters. Being received
with much kindness by Pope Julius, he began in the
chamber of the Segnatura, and painted a picture of
the reconciliation between Philosophy and Astro-
logy, and Theology. He enriched this work with
many figures, and finished it in so delicate and
sweet a manner that Pope Julius caused all the
pictures of the other masters, both ancient and
modern, to be destroyed that Raffaello might have

all the work of the chambers. So Raffaello painted
the ceiling of this chamber with figures of Knowledge,
Poetry, Theology, and Justice, and on the walls were
Parnassus with the Poets, and Heaven with the
saints and doctors of the Church, and Justinian
giving the laws to the doctors, and Pope Julius the
canon laws. And the Pope being satisfied with the
work, gave him the second chamber to paint.

Raffaello had now acquired a great name, having
moreover gentle manners admired by all; but
though he studied continually the antiquities in
the city, he had not yet given to any of his figures
that grandeur and majesty which appeared in his
later works. But it happened at this time that
Michael Angelo, having that difference with the
Pope of which we shall speak in his life, had fled
to Florence, and Bramante, having the key of the
Sistine Chapel, showed it to Raffaello his friend,
that he might learn Michael Angelo's methods.
And this was the cause of his repainting the prophet
Isaiah, which he had already finished in the church
of S. Agostino, greatly improving and elevating his
manner in this work, and giving it more majesty.

Not long after, Agostino Chigi, a very rich merchant of Sienna, entrusted him with the painting of
a chapel, Raffaello having before painted for him in
the loggia of his palace a picture of Galatea. So
Raffaello, having made the cartoon for the chapel
which is in the church of S. Maria della Pace, carried

it out in fresco in his new and grander manner,
painting there some of the Prophets and Sibyls; and
this work is the best and most excellent that he produced in his life.

Continuing then his work in the chambers of the
Vatican, he painted the Miracle of the Mass of
Bolsena and S. Peter in prison, with the punishment
of Heliodorus, and on the ceiling pictures from the
Old Testament. But at this time Pope Julius died,
who had ever been an encourager of talent. Nevertheless Leo X., being created pope, desired the work
to continue, so Raffaello painted the coming of
Attila to Rome, and Pope Leo III. going out to
meet him.

Meanwhile Raffaello painted many other pictures,
and his glory grew great, and the fame of him
reached to France and Flanders, and Albert Dürer,
the great German painter and engraver, sent to
Raffaello a tribute of his own works, a portrait of
himself painted in water-colour on very fine linen,
so that it showed equally on both sides. And Raffaello marvelling at it, sent to him many drawings
from his own hand, which were much prized by
Albert. Also the goldsmith Francesco Francia of
Bologna heard of him, and desired greatly to see
him. For while he was enjoying in peace the glory
he had earned by his labours in Bologna, many
gentlemen of that city going to Rome went to see
Raffaello and his works. And as it is usually the

... ... in ... new and grander ... ...
... ... the Prophets and Sibyls ... ...
... ... and most excellent that ... ...
... ...

... ... when his work in the chapel for the
... ... painted the Miracle of the Mass of
... ... and St. Peter in prison, with the punishment
of Heliodorus, and on the ceiling pictures from the
Old Testament. But at this time Pope Julius ... ...
... Raffaello was an encourager of talent. Nevertheless ... Leo X., being created pope, desired the work
to continue, so Raffaello painted the coming of
Attila to Rome, and Pope Leo III. going out to
meet him.

Meanwhile Raffaello painted many other pictures,
and his glory grew great, and the fame of him
reached to France and Flanders, and Albert Dürer,
the great German painter and engraver, sent to
him ... a tribute to his own works, a portrait of
... ... painted in water-colour on very fine linen
... ... showed equally on both sides. And Raffaello ... looking at it, sent to him many drawings
from his own hand, which were much prized by
Albert. Also the great Flemish Francesco Francia of
Bologna heard of him, and desired greatly to see
him. For ... he had been enjoying in peace the great
... had earned by his labours in Bologna, many
... ... that ... going to Rome, went to see
... ... and his works. And as it is usually the

ABRAHAM AND THE THREE ANGELS. By RAPHAEL.

case that men like to praise to others those of their own house who have talent, so these Bolognese began to talk to Raffaello in praise of Francia's works, and his life and virtues; and so between them there sprang up a kind of friendship, and Francia and Raffaello saluted each other by letter. And Francia hearing of the fame of the divine works of Raffaello, desired much to see them, but being already old was loth to leave his Bologna. Then it happened that Raffaello painted a picture of S. Cecilia, which was to be sent to Bologna and placed in a chapel in S. Giovanni in Monte, and having packed it, he directed it to Francia as his friend that he might set it up in the chapel. At which Francia was very glad, having so long desired to see one of Raffaello's works. And having opened Raffaello's letter (in which he prayed him, if he found it scratched, to mend it, and also, if he saw any error, like a true friend, to correct it), with great delight he drew the picture out of the case and put it in a good light. But so great was his astonishment at what he saw that, recognizing his foolish presumption, he fell sick of grief, and in a short time died. For the picture of Raffaello was divine, not painted but living; and Francia, half dead with the shock, and altogether disheartened by the beauty of the picture compared with those which he saw around him by his own hand, had it placed carefully in the chapel where it was to be, and then in a few days took to his bed, feeling that in art he was nothing compared to what he had thought himself to be and was reputed by others, and died of grief and melancholy. However, some people say that his death was so sudden that it was more like poison or apoplexy.

After this Raffaello painted for the Brothers of Monte Oliveto, in the monastery called S. Maria dello Spasimo of Palermo, a picture of Christ bearing His cross, which when it was finished nearly met with an evil end. For as it was being borne by sea to Palermo, a horrible tempest cast the ship upon a rock, and it was broken to pieces, and all the crew lost, with the merchandize, except this picture, which was carried in its case by the sea to Genoa. Here being drawn to shore, it was seen to be a thing divine, and was taken care of, being found uninjured, even the fury of the winds and waves having respect to the beauty of such a work. When the news of it was spread abroad, the monks sought to regain it, and with the intercession of the Pope obtained it, satisfying the demands of those that saved it. Being carried safe to Sicily, it was placed in Palermo, where it has more reputation than the volcano itself.

While Raffaello was working at these paintings he did not cease to labour in the Pope's chambers, keeping men constantly employed in painting from his designs, and himself overlooking everything.

It was not long, therefore, before he uncovered the chamber of the Borgia Tower, in which he had painted the burning of the Borgo Vecchio of Rome, and Leo IV. stopping it with his blessing, with another picture of the life of St. Leo. The ceiling of this room had been painted by Perugino his master, and Raffaello therefore would not have it destroyed.

He also embellished the other parts of the palace, giving the designs for the staircases and for the loggie which Bramante had begun. And Leo X. wishing to show his great magnificence and generosity, Raffaello made the designs for the ornaments in stucco, and for the pictures to be painted in the loggie, making Giovanni da Udine the chief of the stucco work, and Giulio Romano he set over the figures, though he worked little upon them, Giovan Francesco, called Il Fattore, Perino del Vaga, and others chiefly painting them.

The Pope also, desiring to have some arras woven of gold and silk, Raffaello made some coloured cartoons of the proper form and size with his own hands, which were sent into Flanders to be woven, and when the cloth was finished it was sent back to Rome. For Giulio Cardinal de' Medici he painted the Transfiguration of Christ, which he brought to the greatest perfection, working at it continually with his own hand, and in which it seemed as if he put forth all his strength to show the power of art in the. face of Christ; and having finished it, as the last thing he had to do, he laid aside his pencil, death overtaking him.

So, being seized with a fever, he made his will, and having confessed, he ended his course on the same day that he was born, that is, Good Friday, being thirty-seven years of age.   They placed at the head of the room in which he lay, the picture of the Transfiguration, which he had finished for the Cardinal de' Medici, and all seeing the dead body and the living work were filled with grief.

CHAPTER XVII.

ANDREA DEL SARTO.

ONE of Piero di Cosimo's pupils was Andrea del Sarto, the son of a tailor, who took his name from his father's trade. At the age of seven years he was put with a goldsmith, but Gian Barile, a Florentine painter, seeing his drawings, took him to work with him. After three years' earnest study, Gian Barile perceived that the boy would have extraordinary success if he attended to his studies, and he spoke of him to Piero di Cosimo, who was then considered one of the best painters in Florence, and put him under his care. Andrea, desirous to learn, never rested from his studies, and being a born painter, he managed his colours as if he had worked for fifty years. So Piero loved him much, and was wonderfully pleased to hear that whenever he had time, especially on feast-days, he would spend it in the hall of the Pope, where were the cartoons of Michael Angelo and Lionardo da Vinci, and that he surpassed, though young, all the other artists, natives or strangers, who came constantly to study there. Among these Andrea was most pleased with the conversation of Francia Bigio, and Francia being equally so with Andrea, they became friends ; and Andrea told Francia that he could endure no longer the eccentricities of Piero, who was then getting old, and that he must take a room for himself. Francia being forced to do the same, because Mariotto Albertinelli, his master, had given up painting, proposed that they should join together. So they took a room in the Piazza del Grano, and did many works in company. Afterwards they took new rooms near the convent of the Nunziata, and it happened that Jacopo Sansovino, then a youth, was working in the same place under Andrea Contucci, and he and Andrea formed so close a friendship that they were never apart day or night, and as all their conversation was about art, it is no wonder that they both became excellent masters.

In the convent of the Servites there was a sacristan named Fra Mariano, who constantly hearing Andrea praised and spoken of as one making marvellous progress, thought to get something out of him at little expense. So to try Andrea, who was soft and pliable where honour was concerned, he began to express a wish to help him in a matter which would bring him honour and profit. Now some years before, Cosimo Rosselli had begun in the first cloister a picture of S. Filippo, the founder of the order, taking the habit of monk, but the picture was not finished when he died. The friar, therefore, wishing the rest to be painted, thought by making Andrea and Francia rivals to get it at less expense. So opening his mind to Andrea, he persuaded him to undertake it, pointing out that it was a public place and much frequented, and he would become known to strangers as well as Florentines; he ought not therefore to consider the price, and if he would not do it there was Francia, who had offered to do it and left the price to him. The first suggestions inclined Andrea to undertake it, but when he heard of Francia he resolved at once, and an agreement was made in writing that no one else might interfere. So the friar having set him to work, he was first to finish the life of S. Filippo, having no more than ten ducats for each picture, which the friar said he gave him out of his own money, more for his good than for the profit of the convent. But when he had painted one side of the cloisters, finding the price too little, and that they counted the honour too much, he determined to give up the rest of the work, at which the friar complained greatly and held him to his agreement. So Andrea promised to do two more if he would raise the price. Francia Bigio meanwhile was entrusted with the painting in the cloister of the Servi, and represented the Marriage of the Virgin. The friars, desiring that Andrea's and Francia's pictures should be uncovered for a

certain feast, the night that Francia had finished his
they presumptuously went and uncovered it themselves, not understanding that Francia might retouch
it.   In the morning the news was brought to Francia
that his work and Andrea's had been uncovered,
and it grieved him almost to death.   But falling into
a passion with the friars for their presumption in
showing him so little respect, he rushed to his picture,
and climbing on to the scaffold, which had not yet
been taken down, seized a mason's hammer which
was lying there and struck at some of the women's
faces, spoiling the Virgin's altogether.   The friars
and others running in at the noise held his hands to
prevent his spoiling the whole picture.   But although
they offered him double payment he would never
mend it, and he was so much honoured that no other
would ever finish it.   So the work remained in this
state.

These works brought Andrea into greater notice,
and many pictures and works of importance were
entrusted to him, and he made for himself so great
a name in the city that he was considered one of
the first painters, and although he had asked little
for his works he found himself in a position to help
his relatives.   But falling in love with a young
woman who was left a widow, he took her for his
wife, and had enough to do all the rest of his life,
and had to work harder than he had ever done before,
for besides the duties and liabilities which belong to

certain fact, the most that Francia had meant . . .
. . . y presumptuously went and uncovered it them . . .
. . . ves, not understanding that Francia might . . . . . h
it . . . In the morning the news was brought to Francia
. . . . s work and Andrea's had been uncovered.

. . . . grieved him almost to death. But falling into
. . . . . ssion with the friars for their presumption in
showing him so little respect, he rushed to his picture
and climbing on to the scaffold, which had not yet
been taken down, seized a mason's hammer which
was lying there and struck at some of the Madonna's
faces, spoiling the Virgin's altogether. The friars
and others running in at the noise, held his hands to
prevent his spoiling the whole picture. But although
they offered him double payment he would . . . . er
mend it, and he was so much incensed that never . . .
would ever finish it. So the work remained in this
state.

These works brought Andrea into greater notice,
and many pictures and works of importance we . . .
. . . . to him, and he made for himself so great
a name in the city that he was considered one of
the most painters, and although he had asked little
for his works he found himself in a position to help
his relatives. But falling in love with a young
woman who was left a widow, he took her for his
wife, and had enough to do all the rest of his life,
and had to work harder than he had ever done before;
for besides the cares and liabilities which belong to

STUDY OF A FEMALE HEAD. By ANDREA DEL SARTO.

such a union, he took upon him many more troubles, being constantly, vexed with jealousy and one thing and another. And all who knew his case felt compassion for him, and blamed the simplicity which had reduced him to such a condition. And as he had been much sought after by his friends before, so now he was avoided. For though his pupils stayed with him, hoping to learn something from him, there was not one great or small who did not suffer by her evil words or blows during the time he was there.

Nevertheless, this torment seemed to him the highest pleasure. He never put a woman in any picture which he did not draw from her, for even if another sat to him, through seeing her constantly and having drawn her so often, and, what is more, having her impressed on his mind, it always came about that the head resembled hers.

A certain Florentine, Giovanni Battista Puccini, being extraordinarily pleased with Andrea's work, charged him to paint a picture of our Lady to send to France, but it was so beautiful that he kept it himself and did not send it away. However, trafficking constantly with France, and being employed to send good pictures there, he gave Andrea another picture to paint, of a dead Christ supported by angels. When it was done every one was so pleased with it that Andrea was entreated to let it be engraved in Rome by Agostino Veniziano, but because it did not succeed very well he would never let any

13

other of his pictures be engraved. The picture itself
gave no less pleasure in France than it had done in
Italy, and the king gave orders that Andrea should
do another, on which account he resolved at his
friend's persuasion to go himself to France. But
that year 1515 the Florentines, hearing that Pope
Leo X. meant to honour his native place by a visit,
gave orders that he should be received with great
feasting, and such magnificent decorations were prepared, with arches, statues, and other ornaments, as
had never been seen before, there being at that time
in the city a greater number of men of genius and
talent than there had been before. But what was
most admired was the façade of S. Maria del Fiore,
made of wood and painted with pictures by Andrea
del Sarto, the architecture being by Jacopo Sansovino, with some bas-reliefs and statues, and the
Pope pronounced that it could not have been more
beautiful if it had been in marble.

Meanwhile King Francis I. greatly admiring his
works, was told that Andrea would easily be
persuaded to remove to France and enter into his
service ; and the thing pleased the king well. So he
gave command that money should be paid him for
his journey ; and Andrea set out joyfully for France,
taking with him Andrea Sguazzella his pupil. And
having arrived at the court, he was received lovingly
by the king, and before the first day was over experienced the liberality of that magnanimous king,

receiving gifts of money and rich garments. He
soon began to work, and won the esteem of the king
and the whole court, being caressed by all, so that it
seemed to him he had passed from a state of extreme
unhappiness to the greatest felicity. Among his first
works he painted from life the Dauphin, then only a
few months old, and therefore in swaddling clothes,
and when he brought it to the king he received for it
three hundred crowns of gold. And the king, that he
might stay with him willingly, ordered that great provision should be made for him, and that he should
want for nothing. But one day, while he was working
upon a S. Jerome for the king's mother, there came to
him letters from Lucrezia his wife, whom he had left
in Florence, and she wrote that when he was away,
although his letters told her he was well, she could
not cease from sorrow and constant weeping, using
many sweet words apt to touch the heart of a man
who loved her only too much, so that the poor man
was nearly beside himself when he read that if he
did not return soon he would find her dead. So he
prayed the king for leave to go to Florence and put
his affairs in order, and bring his wife to France,
promising to bring on his return pictures and sculptures of price. The king trusting him gave him
money for this purpose, and Andrea swore on the
Gospels to return in a few months. He arrived in
Florence happily, and enjoyed himself with his beautiful wife and his friends. At last, the time having

come when he ought to return to the king, he found
himself in extremity, for on building and on his
pleasures he had spent his own money and the
king's also.   Nevertheless he would have returned,
but the tears and prayers of his wife prevailed against
his promise to the king.   When he did not return
the king was so angered that for a long time he
would not look at a Florentine painter, and swore
that if ever Andrea fell into his hands, it should be
to his hurt without regard to his talents.

When Frederick II. Duke of Mantua passed through
Florence, going to pay homage to Pope Clement VII.,
he saw over a door in the Medici Palace that portrait
of Pope Leo between Cardinal Giulio de' Medici and
Cardinal de' Rossi, which was made by the great
Raffaello da Urbino.   Being extraordinarily pleased
with it, he considered how he could make it his own,
aud when he was in Rome, choosing his time, he made
request for it from Pope Clement, who granted it him
courteously, and orders were sent to Florence to
Ottaviano de' Medici to put it into a case and send it
to Mantua.   But the thing greatly displeased Ottaviano, who would not have Florence deprived of such
a picture.   He replied therefore that he would not
fail to serve the duke, but that the frame of the
picture being bad, he would have a new one made,
and when it was gilded, he would send the picture
securely to Mantua.   Then Ottaviano, with the view,
as we say, of saving both the goat and its fodder

sent secretly for Andrea and told him how matters stood, and that there was nothing else to be done but to have the picture copied as fast as possible, and send the copy to the duke, secretly keeping the picture from Raffaello's hand. So Andrea promised to do the best he could, and having had a panel made of the same size, he worked at it secretly in Ottaviano's house, and laboured to such effect that, when it was finished, Ottaviano himself, who understood these things well, did not know one from the other, Andrea having even copied some dirty stains that were on the original. So having hidden Raffaello's picture, they sent Andrea's to Mantua, and the duke was perfectly satisfied. Even Giulio Romano the painter, Raffaello's disciple, did not perceive the thing, and would always have believed it to be from Raffaello's hand if Giorgio Vasari (who, being Ottaviano's favourite, had seen Andrea working at the picture) had not discovered the matter to him. For when Giorgio came to Mantua, Giulio paid him much attention, and showed him the antiquities and pictures, and among them this picture of Raffaello's, as the best thing that was there; and Giorgio answered, " The work is most beautiful, but not from the hand of Raffaello." " No ? " said Giulio ; " do not *I* know, who can recognize the touches that I put upon it ? " " You have forgotten," answered Giorgio, " for this is by Andrea del Sarto, and in proof of it look at this sign (showing it to him), which

was put upon it in Florence, because the two being
together were mistaken the one for the other."
When he heard this Giulio had the picture turned
round, and when he saw the countersign, he shrugged
his shoulders and said, " I esteem it none the less
than if it were from Raffaello's hand, rather the more,
for it is a thing beyond nature that a good painter
should imitate so well another's manner and make it
so like."

Not long after, Baldo Magini of Prato, desiring to
have a picture painted for the Madonna della Carcere,
among many other painters Andrea was proposed to
him, and Baldo, though he did not know much about
the matter, was more inclined to him than any other,
and had already intimated to him that he would
employ him, when a Niccolò Soggi of Sansovino,
having friends in Prato, was recommended so strongly
to Baldo that the work was given to him. Nevertheless Andrea's friends sent for him, and he, thinking
certainly the work was to be his, went with Domenico
Puligo and some other painters his friends to Prato.
But when he arrived he found that Niccolò had not
only turned Baldo against him, but was himself so
daring and insolent as to propose in the presence of
Baldo that they should make a wager who could
paint the best picture. Andrea, knowing what Niccolò
was worth, answered (though he was generally a
man of little spirit), " I have this pupil of mine with
me who has not been studying long, if you like to

have a wager with him, I will put down the money
for him ; but for nothing will I consent to wager
with you, for if I were to win, it would be no honour
to me, and if I lost, it would be the greatest disgrace."
Then telling Baldo that he did right to give the work
to Niccolò, for he would do it so that it would please
people going to market, he returned to Florence.

Here he was employed by Giacomo, a Servite
friar, who, when absolving a woman from a vow,
had commanded her to have the figure of our Lady
painted over a door in the Nunziata. Finding
Andrea, he told him that he had this money to
spend, and although it was not much, it would be
well done of him to undertake it ; and Andrea, being
soft-hearted, was prevailed upon by the father's
persuasions, and painted in fresco our Lady with the
Child in her arms, and St. Joseph leaning on a sack.
This picture needs none to praise it, for all can see it
to be a most rare work.

One day Andrea had been painting the intendant
of the monks of Vallombrosa, and when the work
was done some of the colour was left over, and
Andrea, taking a tile, called Lucrezia, his wife, and
said, "Come here, for as this colour is left, I will
paint you, that it may be seen how well you are
preserved for your age, and yet how you have changed
and how different you are from your first portraits."
But the woman, having some fancy or other, would
not sit still, and Andrea, as if he guessed that he

was near his end, took a mirror and painted himself instead so well that the portrait seems alive. This portrait is still in possession of Lucrezia his wife.

During the siege of Florence some of the captains of the city escaped, carrying with them the pay of their soldiers; therefore Andrea was charged to paint them in the Piazza del Podestà, together with some other citizens who had escaped and become rebels. That he might not be nicknamed Andrea of the Hanged Men, as Andrea dal Castagno had been, he gave it out that one of his pupils, Bernardo del Buda, was doing it; but, having enclosed the place with a hoarding, he used to go in and out by night, and carried out the work with his own hand so well that the figures appeared alive. The paintings on the façade of the old Mercatanzia were many years afterwards covered with whitewash that they might not be seen.

After the siege was over, Florence was filled with the soldiers from the camp, and some of the spearmen being ill with the plague caused no little panic in the city, and in a short time the infection spread. Either from the fear excited by it, or from having committed some excess in eating after the privations of the siege, Andrea one day fell ill, and having taken to his bed, he died, it is said, almost without any one perceiving it, without medicine and without much care, for his wife kept as far from him as she could for fear of the plague.

CHAPTER XVIII.

MATURINO AND POLIDORO AND MONSIGNORI.

In that age of gold, as we may call the happy age
of Leo X., among the most noble minds Polidoro
da Caravaggio has an honourable place. He came
to Rome about the time when the loggie of the
Pope's palace were being built under the direction of
Raffaello, and until he was eighteen years of age
was employed in carrying the bricklayer's hod for
the builders. But when the painting began Polidoro's desires turned to painting, and he grew intimate with all the young men of talent that he might
learn their method of working. But from among
them all he chose for a companion Maturino, a
Florentine, with whom he worked, taking so much
pleasure in the art that in a few months he did things
which astonished every one who had known him in
his former condition. And the love of Maturino for
Polidoro, and Polidoro's for Maturino, grew so strong
that they resolved to live and die together like brothers, and having their work and money in common,

they set themselves to work together. And because Baldassare of Sienna had been doing the façades of some houses in chiaroscuro they determined to follow his example. They began, therefore, to study the antiquities of Rome, and copied the ancient marbles until they both alike acquired the antique style, and the one so like the other that as their minds were moved by the same will, so their hands expressed the same knowledge. Of what great use they have been to the art of painting may be seen by the number of foreign artists who continually study their works; for all artists in Rome copy the pictures of Polidoro and Maturino more than all the other modern paintings. Nevertheless they could never give that beauty to works in colour which they constantly gave to works in chiaroscuro, or in bronze or clay, and some children which they painted in colours in S. Agostino in Rome do not seem to have come from the hands of illustrious men, but rather to have been done by some simpletons learning to paint. But if I were to name all their works, I should have to make a whole book of the doings of these two men, for there is no house or palace or garden or vineyard where there are not works by Polidoro and Maturino.

But now while Rome in smiles was embellishing herself with their works, and they were looking for the reward of their labours, envious fortune sent the Constable Bourbon to Rome, who in the year 1527 sacked the city. By this not only Maturino and

Polidoro were separated, but many thousands of friends and relatives. Maturino, taking flight, had not gone far when he died of the plague, and was buried in S. Eustachio. Polidoro took his way to Naples, but finding the nobles there little curious in matters of art, he was like to die of hunger, and was forced to support life by working for other painters. Seeing, therefore, that the people of Naples took more account of a horse that could jump than of a man who could paint figures that seemed alive, he went on board a galley and departed to Messina, where he found more honour and produced many works, which are scattered in different places.

When Charles V. returned from his victory at Tunis he passed through Messina, and Polidoro made some very fine triumphal arches, by which he earned a name and great rewards. And he in whom burnt always the desire to see again that Rome for which those who have lived there many years always pine, set himself to paint, as his last picture, Christ bearing His Cross, after which he resolved to depart from that country, although he was held in good account there; and he took out of the bank a good sum of money that he had and prepared to set out. Now Polidoro had had in his service for a long time a boy of the country, who bore greater love to Polidoro's money than to himself, but because he kept it in the bank he had never been able to touch it. But now a wicked and cruel thought came into his mind, and

he resolved with the aid of some of his friends to
put his master to death the next night while he was
sleeping, and to share his money with them. So they
set upon him while he was in his first sleep and
strangled him with a cord, and afterwards inflicted
many wounds upon him, and to show it was not they
who had done it, they carried him to the door of a
house where dwelt a lady whom Polidoro loved, that
it might be supposed it was her kinsman who had
slain him.

Then the boy, having given a good part of the
money to the ruffians who had aided him and sent
them away, went weeping to the house of a count
who was a friend of his dead master, and told him
what had happened, and a diligent search was made
for those who had done the treacherous deed; but
nothing came to light. At last, as Heaven would
have it, one who had no interest in the matter
chanced to say that it was impossible that any
one but the boy himself could have assassinated
him. Upon that the count caused him to be
seized and put to the torture, when he confessed
his crime and was condemned to the gallows.
But this would not give back life to Polidoro.
So they celebrated his obsequies with solemn ceremonies, and with the infinite grief of all Messina
he was buried in the cathedral.

There have always flourished in Verona from the
time of Fra Giocondo men excellent in painting

and architecture, such as Francesco Monsignori, who
being encouraged by his father to apply himself to
drawing, went to Mantua to find Mantegna, who was
working in that city. He laboured so unweariedly,
spurred on by the fame of his preceptor, that it was
not long before Francesco II., Marquis of Mantua,
who delighted in every kind of painting, took him
into his service, gave him a house in Mantua to live
in, and assigned him an honourable provision.
Francesco was not ungrateful for these benefits, and
served this lord with the greatest fidelity and affection, and the marquis, on his side, grew daily more
fond of him, until at last he never left the city without Francesco, and was heard to say that Francesco
was dearer to him than his whole state.

One day the marquis was watching him while he
was working upon a picture of S. Sebastian, and
said to him, " Francesco, you must have a finely
formed model for this saint ? " And Francesco replied,
" I am drawing from a porter with a very fine figure,
and I tie him up, as I want him to make my work
natural." And the marquis answered, " But the
limbs of your saint do not look right, for they do not
seem to be drawn by force ; and there is not that
terror which one would imagine in a man who is tied
up and being shot at, but if you like, I will show you
what you should do to make the figure right." " I
pray you to do so, my lord," said Francesco. And
he answered, " When you have tied up your porter

send for me, and I will show you what you ought to do." So the next day Francesco tied him up as he wanted him and sent secretly to call the marquis, not knowing what he meant to do. Then the marquis rushed into the room in a fury, with a loaded cross-bow in his hand and ran at the porter, crying aloud, " Traitor, you are a dead man ; I have caught you as I wanted," and other like words, and the poor fellow hearing them, and thinking himself a dead man, struggled to free himself from the ropes with which he was bound, and in his panic fear represented truly the horror of death in his face and in his distorted limbs. Then the marquis said to Francesco, " There, that is how he should be ; the rest you must do yourself." And the painter considering the matter, gave his figure all the perfection that could be imagined.

The Grand Turk had sent by one of his men a present to the marquis of a very fine dog, a bow, and a quiver. Thereupon the marquis set Francesco to paint the dog and the man who had brought it and the other things; and when it was done, wishing to see if the dog was lifelike, he caused one of his own dogs, who was a great enemy to the Turkish dog, to be brought into the room where the dog was painted, standing on a stone pavement. And as soon as the live dog saw the painted one standing as if it were alive, and just like the one whom he mortally hated, he threw himself upon it to seize it, breaking away from the man who held him, and striking his head with such force against the wall that he dashed his skull to pieces.

Benedetto Baroni, Francesco's nephew, had a picture of his, about which a story has been told by some people who were present. It was a picture of little more than two spans in length, a half-length of the Madonna, and at her side the Child from His shoulder upwards, with His arm lifted in the act of caressing His mother, and it is said that when the Emperor was master of Verona, Don Alonzo of Castile, and Alarcone, the famous captain, were in that city, and being in the house of Count Lodovico da Sesso, said that they should like very much to see this picture. So having sent for it, they were standing one evening looking at it in a good light and admiring the skill of the work, when the count's wife, the Lady Caterina, came by with one of her sons, who had in his hand one of those green birds which are called in Verona "terrazzani," because they make their nest on the ground, and which will perch on your wrist like a hawk. It happened then that while she was standing with the others looking at the picture this bird, seeing the outstretched arm of the painted Child, flew up to perch upon it, and not being able to attach itself to the picture, fell down, but twice it returned, thinking it was one of the living children who were always carrying it on their wrists. The lords, greatly astonished, would

have paid Benedetto a great price to have had the
picture, but they could not get it from him by any
means. And when, not long after, they planned to
steal it from him at a feast, he was warned of it, and
their design did not succeed.

Francesco was a man of holy life, and an enemy
of vice, so that he would never paint any evil pictures
though the marquis many times prayed him. And
his brothers were like him in goodness. The third,
who was a friar of the Observantines of S. Dominic,
called Fra Girolamo, was also a reasonably good
painter. He was a person of most simple habits,
and quite a stranger to the things of the world. He
lived at a farm belonging to the convent, and that he
might escape all trouble and disturbance, he kept the
money which was sent him for his work, and which
he used for buying colours and such things, in an
uncovered box hanging to a beam in the middle of
his room, so that any one could take it. And that he
might not have trouble every day about his food, he
used on Monday to cook a saucepan of beans to last
him the week. When the plague came to Mantua,
and the sick were abandoned, as has often happened
in such cases, Fra Girolamo, moved only by the
highest charity, would not leave the poor sick fathers,
but served them with his own hands, and so, caring
not that for the love of God he lost his own life, he
took the infection and died, to the grief of all who
knew him.

CHAPTER XIX.

IL ROSSO.

THE Florentine painter Il Rosso, who was honoured above every one of his trade by so great a king as the King of France, was endowed with many gifts besides that of painting. For he was a man of splendid presence, with a gracious and serious manner of speaking, being a good musician, with a knowledge of philosophy. In architecture also he was excellent, and always, however poor he might be, he showed himself rich and great in soul. In his youth he drew from Michael Angelo's cartoon in the Council Hall, but would have little to do with any masters. Having obtained some reputation by his works, he was entrusted with the painting of a picture which Raffaello had left unfinished. He also painted for Gio. Bandini a story from the life of Moses, which I think was sent to France. Another for Cavalcanti, who was going to England, was of Jacob at the well. Il Rosso was living while he was at work upon it in the Borgo de' Tintori

14

which joins on to the garden of the friars of S. Croce,
and he was at that time much attached to a monkey,
which had the nature of a man rather than an animal.
He kept him always with him, and loved him as
himself, and because he had a marvellous understanding, he taught him to perform many services.
The animal attached himself to one of his lads
named Battistino, who was very beautiful, and he
seemed to understand everything he wanted him to
do.   Now against the back of the house which looked
out on the friars' garden, there was a trellis covered
with a vine full of great San Colombo grapes, and
the young fellows used to send the monkey down
and draw him up again by a rope with his hands full
of grapes.   The friar, who had the charge of the
vines, finding his vines getting thinned and suspect-
ing the mice, kept watch, and discovered Il Rosso's
monkey descending.   Full of rage, he snatched up a
stick and ran towards him to beat him.   The monkey
seeing that if he began to climb, he would catch him,
and the same if he stood still, began leaping about in
a way that threatened to bring down the vine, and
took hold of the trellis, intending to throw himself
on the friar's back.   At the same moment the
friar waved his stick, and the monkey in his terror
shook the trellis so violently that the beams gave
way, and trellis and monkey and all came down on
the top of the friar, who cried out for mercy, while
Battistino and the others pulled the monkey up safe

into their room. The friar meanwhile went off in a
rage, and proceeded in great anger to the office of the
Council of Eight, magistrates who were much feared
in Florence. Having lodged his complaint, Il Rosso
was summoned, and the monkey was jokingly condemned to have a weight attached to him that he
might not be able to jump about as he had done. So
Il Rosso made a roller which turned on a iron bar, so
that he might go about the house, but not climb into
other people's gardens. The monkey, finding himself condemned to such a piece of torture, seemed to
guess that the friar was the cause of it ; he set to
work therefore, and practised himself every day in
leaping, carrying the weight in his hands, until at
last he was ready for his design. Then one day,
being left loose by accident, he leaped from roof to
roof until he came to the friar's own room, just at
the hour when the friar was at vespers. Then drop-
ing the weight, he had such a merry dance on the
roof for half an hour that there was not a tile that
was not broken when he returned to the house.

When Il Rosso had finished his work he went off
with Battistino and the monkey to Rome, where
great things were expected of him, for some of his
drawings had been seen which were considered
marvellous. He produced one work in the Pace
above Raffaello's paintings, but he never painted
anything worse in all his life; nor can I imagine how
this came about unless it was the change of place.

It may be that with the air of Rome and the astounding things that he saw, the architecture and sculpture, and the pictures and statues of Michael Angelo, he was not himself; in the same way that Fra Bartolommeo and Andrea del Sarto fled from Rome without leaving any works behind them. Whatever was the cause, Il Rosso never did worse, and moreover the painting has to stand comparison with Raffaello's.

When the sack of Rome happened, poor Il Rosso was made prisoner by the Germans, and very badly treated, for having stripped him of his clothes, they made him go barefoot and bareheaded carrying heavy weights, until he succeeded in escaping to Perugia. Afterwards he came to Arezzo, and was entrusted with a painting in fresco in the Madonna delle Lagrime. But when the siege of Florence began in 1530, the people of Arezzo looked with an evil eye upon the Florentines, and Il Rosso would not trust himself to them, and went away to Borgo S. Sepolcro, leaving the cartoons and the drawings for the work shut up in the citadel, and he would never return but finished the picture there.

He had always had a desire to end his life in France, and escape, as he said, from the certain misery and poverty which befal men who work in Tuscany, and in the lands where they are born; so he determined now to depart, and studied for that purpose the Latin language that he might take a better position. He was forced however to hasten his

departure, for on Holy Thursday, being in church
with a young Aretine who was a pupil of his, the
young fellow, with a candle and some pitch, produced
some flames while they were holding the service of
the Tenebræ, for which he was reproached and
somewhat knocked about by some of the priests. Il
Rosso, who was sitting by the side of the boy, perceiving this, started up angrily in the priest's face,
which occasioned a disturbance, and no one knowing
exactly what was the matter, all rushed sword in hand
against poor Il Rosso, who was struggling with the
priests. He betook himself to flight, and dexterously
made his escape to his abode without being hurt.
However, considering himself insulted, he set off at
night, and went by the way of Pesaro to Venice and
thence to France, where he was received with many
caresses by the Florentines there.

He presented some pictures to King Francis which
pleased him greatly, but still more did his presence
and bearing and conversation; for he was tall in
person, of a red complexion, agreeing with his name,
and in all his gestures grave and judicious. The
king therefore immediately ordered him a provision
of four hundred crowns, and gave him a house in
Paris, where however he lived but little, spending
most of his time at Fontainebleau. He also set him
over all the buildings and pictures of that place, and
he adorned it with paintings which pleased the king
so greatly that it was not long before he gave him

a canonry in the chapel of the Madonna at Paris, with other gifts, so that Il Rosso lived like a lord, with a great number of servants and horses, and gave banquets to all his friends and acquaintances, especially to the Italians, and had his house supplied with tapestry and silver and furniture of value. But fortune, which seldom or never leaves in their glory those who trust too much in her, brought him most strangely to a miserable end. For while Francesco di Pellegrino, a Florentine, was working with him familiarly, being one who delighted greatly in painting, and a great friend of Il Rosso's, it happened that Il Rosso was robbed of some hundreds of ducats, and not knowing whom to suspect except this Francesco, he caused him to be brought before the courts and subjected to a rigorous examination and put to the torture. But he confessing nothing was found innocent and let go free, and moved by a just anger, resented the injurious charge with which he had been falsely accused, and summoning Il Rosso in his turn, pressed his complaint in such a manner that Il Rosso, not knowing how to defend himself, found himself in evil case. For he had not only falsely accused his friend, but had stained his own honour. So he determined rather to kill himself than be punished by others. One day therefore, when the king was at Fontainebleau, he sent a man to Paris for a certain poison, representing that he wanted to use it for his colours or varnishes. The man while returning with it held his thumb over the mouth of the bottle, which however was stopped with wax, but such was the malignity of the poison that he almost lost his finger, which was as it were eaten away by it. Il Rosso himself taking it in a few hours cut short his life. The news being brought to the king displeased him greatly, for it seemed to him that by his death he had lost the greatest artist of his time.

CHAPTER XX.

PARMIGIANO.

AMONG the many in Lombardy who have been
endowed with a gift for drawing and a spirit of invention and a talent for painting beautiful landscapes,
none is to be put before Francesco Mazzuoli Parmi-
giano. If he had only kept to the study of painting,
and not gone after the nonsense of congealing mercury to make himself rich, he would have been without compare. Francesco was born in Parma in 1504,
and his father dying when he was a child of tender
age, he was left in the custody of two old uncles,
both painters, who brought him up with the greatest
love, and taught him all that a Christian and a
citizen ought to know. He had no sooner taken a
pen into his hand to learn to write than he began to
draw marvellously, and his master perceiving this,
persuaded his uncles to let him apply himself to
painting. They, although they were old and painters
of no great fame, were men of good judgment, and
placed him under excellent masters. And because

they found that he had been born, as they say, with
a pencil in his hand, sometimes they urged him on,
and sometimes fearing that too much study would
injure his health, they restrained him. At length
having reached the age of sixteen, he completed a
picture of S. John baptizing Christ, which even now
causes astonishment that a boy could have done such
a thing.

Many others he painted before he attained the age
of nineteen. Then came upon him the desire to see
Rome, hearing men greatly praise the works of the
masters there, especially of Raffaello and Michael
Angelo, and he told his desire to his old uncles.
They seeing nothing in the desire that was not
praiseworthy, agreed, but said that it would be well
to take something with him which would gain him
an introduction to artists. And the counsel seeming
good to Francesco, he painted three pictures, two
small and one very large. Besides these, inquiring
one day into the subtleties of art, he began to draw
himself as he appeared in a barber's convex glass.
He had a ball of wood made at a turner's and divided
in half, and on this he set himself to paint all that
he saw in the glass, and because the mirror enlarged
everything that was near and diminished what was
distant, he painted the hand a little large. Francesco
himself, being of very beautiful countenance and more
like an angel than a man, his portrait on the ball
seemed a thing divine, and the work altogether was

a happy success, having all the lustre of the glass, with every reflection and the light and shade so true that nothing more could be hoped for from the human intellect.

The pictures being finished and packed, together with the portrait, he set out, accompanied by one of his uncles, for Rome; and as soon as the Chancellor of the Pope had seen the pictures, he introduced the youth and his uncle to Pope Clement, who seeing the works produced and Francesco so young, was astonished, and all his court with him. And his Holiness gave him the charge of painting the Pope's hall.

. Francesco studying in Rome wished to see everything ancient and modern, sculpture and painting, that there was in the city; but he held in special veneration the works of Michael Angelo and Raffaello da Urbino, and people said when they saw this youth of such rare art and such gentle, graceful manners, that the spirit of Raffaello had passed into the body of Francesco, seeing also that he strove to imitate him in everything, especially in painting, and not in vain.

But while he was painting a picture for S. Salvadore del Lauro came the ruin and the sack of Rome, which not only banished all art for the time, but cost the lives of many artists, and Francesco was very near losing his; for at the beginning of the tumult he was so intent on his work that when the soldiers began entering the houses — and some

Germans were already in his—he, for all the noise they made, did not move from his place. But they coming suddenly upon him, and seeing his painting, were so astonished by it that, like good fellows, they let him alone. And while the poor city was ruined by the impious cruelty of the barbarians, sacred and profane things alike suffering, without respect to God or man, he was taken care of by these Germans, and honoured and defended from injury. All the annoyance that he suffered from them was that, one of them being a great connoisseur in painting, he was forced to make a number of drawings in water-colour or in pen and ink, which were taken as the payment of his ransom. But on the soldiers being changed, Francesco fell into trouble, for while he was going to look for some friends, he was made prisoner by some other soldiers, and obliged to give up the few crowns he had. His uncle, seeing that all hope of Francesco's acquiring knowledge, fame, and wealth was cut off, and that Rome was little less than ruined, and the Pope a prisoner in the hands of the Spaniards, determined to take him back to Parma.

But having reached Bologna, and meeting there many friends, he stayed some months in that city, and caused some of his works to be engraved, having with him for that purpose one Antonio da Trento. But this Antonio one morning when Francesco was in bed opened a chest, took out all

the engravings and woodcuts, and whatever drawings he could find, and took himself off it was never
known where; and though Francesco recovered the
engravings, which the fellow had left with a friend,
intending probably to get them when it was convenient, he never saw his drawings again. Half
desperate, he returned to his painting, and was
forced for the sake of earning some money to paint
the portrait of some Bolognese Count or other.

When the Emperor Charles V. came to Bologna
that Clement VII. might crown him, Francesco
went to see him dine, and without drawing his
portrait painted a very large picture of this Cæsar,
with Fame crowning him with laurel. And when
it was finished, he showed it to Pope Clement,
and it pleased him so much that he sent both the
picture and Francesco to the emperor, accompanied
by the bishop of Verona. The picture pleasing his
Majesty also, he gave him to understand that he was
to leave it; but Francesco, by the counsel of a not
very faithful or not very wise friend, said it was not
finished, and so his Majesty did not have it, and he
was not rewarded as he certainly would have been.

So Francesco, after many years' absence from his
home, in which he had gained experience in art, and
had acquired friends but no wealth, returned at last
to Parma. And immediately he was set to paint in
fresco in the church of S. Maria della Steccata.
He was also employed in painting a picture for a

gentleman of Parma, and for the church of S. Maria
de' Servi. But it soon appeared that he was neg-
lecting the work in the Steccata, or at least doing
it so much at his ease, that it was evident things
were going badly with him ; and this was because
he had begun to study alchemy, and to put aside for
it his painting, hoping to enrich himself quickly
by congealing mercury. So using his brains no
longer for thinking out fine conceptions, and over
his pencils and colours, he lost all his days instead'
over his charcoal and wood and glass bottles and
such trash, spending more in a day than he earned
in a week by his painting in the Steccata, and having
no other means, he began to find that his furnaces
were ruining him little by little. And what was
worse still, the company of the Steccata, seeing that
he neglected his work, and having perhaps paid him
beforehand, began a suit against him. He therefore
fled by night with some of his friends to Casal
Maggiore, where, putting his alchemy for a while out
of his head, he returned to his painting, and made a
Lucretia, which was the best thing that had ever
been seen from his hand. But his mind was constantly turning to his alchemy, and he himself was
changed from the gentle, delicate youth to a savage
with long, ill-kept hair and beard, and in this melancholy state he was attacked by a fever, which carried
him off in a few days.

CHAPTER XXI.

PERINO DEL VAGA.

THERE was in the city of Florence one Giovanni Buonaccorsi, who being young and high-spirited, joined the service of Charles VIII., and spent all his property in the wars and in gambling. To him was born a son named Piero, whose mother died of the plague when he was only two months old, and he was brought up in great poverty, being fed with goat's milk, until his father going to Bologna took as his second wife a woman who had lost her first husband and her sons of the plague. She nursed the little Piero, calling him by the pet name of Pierino, and this name clung to him always. His father afterwards brought him to Florence and left him with some of his relations there, when he returned to France. He was taken as he grew older by Andrea de' Ceri, a painter, who was pleased with his ways and looks. Andrea was a very ordinary painter, and kept an open shop, working in public all sorts of mechanical things, and he used to paint some tapers every year for the feast of S. John, by which he obtained the name of Andrea de' Ceri, and Perino for a time was known as Perino de' Ceri. Andrea kept Perino for some years, and taught him to the best of his power the principles of art, but was forced when he reached the age of eleven years to put him with a better master, and being intimate with Ridolfo son of Domenico Ghirlandaio, who had many youths in his workshop, he put Perino with him. There was one among them named Toto del Nunziata, who was a continual spur to urge him on, and Perino competing with him was not long in becoming an excellent scholar.

There came at that time to Florence Il Vaga the Florentine, who was working in Toscanella, and though he was not an excellent master, work was abundant with him, and he needed helpers. Therefore seeing Perino working in Ridolfo's workshop, and superior to the other scholars, being also a beautiful youth, and courteous, modest, and gentle, he asked him if he would go with him to Rome. Perino had such a great desire to attain a high rank in his profession that when he heard of Rome his heart glowed, but he said he must speak to Andrea de' Ceri, for he would not abandon him who had helped him till that time. So Vaga persuaded Ridolfo and Andrea to let him go, and took him with him to Toscanella, where he began to work, and Perino to help him. But when Perino lamented that the promise of taking him to Rome was delayed, and determined to go by himself, Vaga left his work and took him himself to Rome ; and when he would return to Toscanella he recommended Perino to all the friends he had that they might help him, and so from that time forward he was always called Perino del Vaga.

Perino, therefore, burning with his love of art and his desire to become great in it, was forced to work like a day labourer, now with one painter and now with another, but finding this very inconvenient for his studies, he determined to work half the week for pay, and to give the other half to study, reserving also all the feast days and a great part of the nights. So he studied in the Pope's chapel, following the manner of Raffaello, and learnt how to work in stucco, and copied ancient marbles, stinting himself to the utmost and begging his bread, that he might through any misery become excellent in his profession. And before long he became the best draughtsman among those who were studying in Rome, and Giulio Romano and Giovan Francesco, called Il Fattore, made him known to their master, Raffaello. Now Raffaello was then working at the loggie that Leo X. had ordered, and he had chosen in Rome or brought thither many masters, a company of men of worth, to work, some in stucco, some in grotesques, some on leaves, festoons, and such things, and as he found that any one did well, he brought him forward and gave him better wages, and by this means many youths were

perfected who afterwards were well known. Into
this company Perino was brought, and soon showed
himself the best for drawing and colour. He always
showed submission and reverent obedience towards
Raffaello, so that he was loved by him as his own son.
And his name becoming known, he was employed
by others, having already accomplished many works
in Rome and made himself famous.

In the year 1523 the plague broke out in Rome,
and Perino, that he might save his life, determined
to leave; and Piloto the goldsmith, a friend of
Perino's, being at table with him one day, persuaded him to go with him to Florence. It was
many years since he had been there, but although
Andrea de' Ceri and his wife were dead, it was
still dear to him as the place of his birth. So
it was not long before he and Piloto set off one
morning and came to Florence. And being arrived
there, he found the greatest pleasure in looking
again at the old things painted by masters long
dead, which had been his study in his childish
years, and also in seeing the works of the masters
then living.

One day it happened that many artists, sculptors,
architects, and goldsmiths, having met together according to the old custom to do him honour, some
wishing to see Perino and hear what he had to say,
and some wanting to see what was the difference
between the artists of Rome and those of Florence

in their methods of working, it happened, I say, that
while they were talking of one thing and another,
they came to the church of the Carmine to see
Masaccio's chapel. And each one considering it
attentively, and adding his mite to the praise of this
great master, all affirmed that it was marvellous
that he who had seen nothing but Giotto's paintings
should have worked in so modern a style, and that
even now there was no one who could equal him in
relief and in execution. This conversation pleased
Perino well, and he replied to the artists, " I do not
deny that what you say is true, and much more besides, but that no one has equalled his manner, I
deny ; rather, I should say, that I know many a one
whose style is bolder and more graceful, and I, who
am not among the first in art—I am sorry that there
is no room here for me to paint a figure by the side
of one of these in fresco, that you may see if there
is no one among the moderns who can equal him."
There was present a master who was considered the
first in Florence, and he being curious to see Perino's
work, and perhaps desirous to lower his pride, said,
" Although this side is full, yet as you have such a
desire—certainly a good and praiseworthy one—there
is a space on the other side where his S. Paul is, and
you can easily show us what you say, by painting
another apostle by the side either of Masolino's
S. Peter or Masaccio's S. Paul." The S. Peter was
nearest the window, and there was more space there

and better light, while it was as fine a figure as the
S. Paul. So they all urged Perino to do it, because
they wanted to see this Roman manner, and many
said he would be the means of ridding their minds of
a fancy which they had held to for scores of years,
and if his was better they would all run after the
modern things. So Perino was persuaded at last by
hearing one of the masters say that he might paint a
figure in fresco in a fortnight, and they would spend
years in praising it, and he resolved to make the
attempt. And the prior of the convent was called,
and courteously gave them leave to paint in the
place. And they took the measure of the space, the
height and the width, and departed.

Then Perino made a cartoon, choosing the apostle
S. Andrew, and finished it carefully, and had the
scaffolding prepared for painting it. But before his
coming some of his friends, who had seen his works
in Rome, had procured for him a commission for a
painting in fresco. There were a number of men
in the Camaldoli in Florence who had formed themselves into a company called the Company of the
Martyrs; and they desired to have painted the story
of those martyrs who having been taken in battle
were condemned by the two Roman emperors to be
crucified. And this had been entrusted to Perino,
who undertook it gladly, although the price was
small, for he thought it would bring him the consideration he deserved among the citizens and artists

in Florence.   He made therefore a small drawing,
which was pronounced divine, and then began a
cartoon as large as the work.   And when this was
seen, all said that nothing equal in beauty and drawing had been seen since Michael Angelo had made
his cartoon for the Council Hall.

Now Perino had long been friendly with a Ser
Raffaello di Sandro, a priest of S. Lorenzo, and he
persuaded him to take up his quarters with him, and
Perino lodged there many weeks.   But the plague
began to show itself in certain places in Florence,
and Perino for fear of it determined to depart.   He
wished first however to remunerate Ser Raffaello,
but he would not consent to take anything, saying,
" A scrap of paper from your hand would be enough."
So Perino took a thick piece of cloth about four
braccia in size, and fixed it to a wall, and painted on
it in bronze colour in one day and one night the
Crossing of the Red Sea.   And this he gave to Ser
Raffaello, who was as glad of it as if he had made
him prior of S. Lorenzo.

Then Perino departed from Florence, leaving unfinished the Martyrs to his great regret, and if it had
been in any other place than the Camaldoli he would
have finished it, but that convent had been set apart
for the infected, and he would rather save his life
than leave a fame of himself in Florence, having
already shown by his drawings what he was worth.

For many months he fled from place to place to

escape the plague, but when it had ceased he returned to Rome. Now after the death of Raffaello it had been resolved to make Giulio Romano and Giovan Francesco, called Il Fattore, chiefs of the works, that they might divide the work among the other painters; but Perino showed himself so excellent that they did not doubt he would be placed above them, being also a disciple of Raffaello. They therefore determined to attach him to their interests, and gave him the sister of Giovan Francesco to wife, and thus changed their friendship into kinship.

And this lasted until in the year 1527 came the ruin of Rome, and Perino, with his wife and his little girl hanging on his neck, ran about from place to place seeking a shelter, and at last was made prisoner. And they made him pay such a sum for his ransom that he was nearly out of his mind; and even after the fury of the sack was over, he was so much overwhelmed by his ruin that he could do nothing with his art. But Il Baviera, who was the only one who had not lost much, made him draw for him the Metamorphoses of the Gods, which was engraved by Jacopo Caraglio.

But while he was in such misery there came to Rome Niccola Veniziano, a servant of Prince Doria's, and he out of old friendship for Perino persuaded him to go to Genoa, promising him that the prince, who was a lover of painting, would give him work; and Perino was not hard to persuade. So leaving his

wife and child with their relatives in Rome, he set
out for Genoa, and was received with great kindness
by the prince. And the prince determined to make
a palace adorned with stucco and with pictures in
fresco and oil; and there Perino produced those
works which are his best.

It is said that before his coming Girolamo da
Trevigi had been painting there, and when he saw
Perino making cartoons and sketches on different
sheets of papers, and not beginning the work itself,
he began to raise a complaint against him, saying,
"Cartoons, nothing but cartoons! I carry my art
at the end of my brush." These words came to
Perino's ears, and being angry, he caused his cartoon
to be fixed on the ceiling where he was to paint,
and taking away some of the scaffolding that it
might be seen from below, he opened the hall. And
all Genoa ran to see the picture, and were astonished
at it. And among them came Girolamo da Trevigi,
and seeing what he had never expected to see from
Perino's hand, terrified by its beauty, he departed
from Genoa, without even taking leave of Prince
Doria, and returned to Bologna.

So Perino proceeded with his work, and adorned
many of the rooms with his paintings, and decorated
the poops of Prince Doria's galleys, and made many
banners and standards, so that he was much loved
by the prince, and would have been greatly rewarded
by him. But while he was working there the fancy

took him to fetch his wife from Rome, and to buy
himself a house in Pisa, thinking as he was growing
old to settle there. But remembering Rome in the
happy days of Leo, he desired greatly to return, and
one morning the whim took him and he left Pisa and
went to Rome.

Nevertheless for some months he was left without
employment, and was tempted to depart again; but
his friends comforted him, and bade him have patience, saying that Rome was no longer what she
had been. And after a time he was employed in the
chapel of the Pope, where Michael Angelo painted
the Last Judgment, and by degrees much work
came into his hands.

But in his last works he followed the example of
Raffaello, and the designing of his works pleasing
him more than the completing of them, he gave them
to others to carry out. He however who would
preserve his name should do the whole work himself. But Perino had so many things entrusted to
him that he was forced to employ others, besides he
had now a thirst for gain rather than glory, having
prospered so ill in his youth. He acquired such an
influence that almost all the work in Rome was
entrusted to him. But he had taken upon himself
too great a burden, being infirm. He had to work
day and night, not only at great works, but at drawings for embroidery, carving, and all kinds of ornaments, so that he had not an hour of repose, except

when he sat with his friends at the tavern, which he held to be the true blessedness of life. So, worn out with his labours and the disorders of his life, he fell into a consumption, and one evening while talking to a friend near his house he fell dead, at the age of forty-seven.

CHAPTER XXII.

BACCIO BANDINELLI.

IN the days when art flourished at Florence, under the favour of the magnificent Lorenzo de' Medici, there was in the city a goldsmith named Michael Angelo di Viviano da Gaiuole, who worked excellently with his chisel, and was skilled in niello work, and had great knowledge of jewels, so that his shop was considered the first in Florence. He was also very familiar with the sons of Lorenzo, and when the Medici fled from Florence in the year 1494, they left with him much plate and treasure, which he kept secretly and restored faithfully when they returned. To him was born a son whom he named Bartolommeo, but who was always called, after the manner of Florence, Baccio. And as in those times no one was thought to be a good goldsmith who was not a good draughtsman and could not work well in relief, he put him with other boys to learn drawing. While Baccio was still a child he was one day in the shop of Girolamo

del Bada, on the Piazza of S. Pulinari, and there had
been a heavy fall of snow, which had been piled up
in heaps. Girolamo turning to Baccio said to him
in jest, "Baccio, if that snow were marble we might
carve out of it a great giant like Marforio lying
down." "So we might," said Baccio, "let us treat
it as if it were marble." So putting on his cloak
he set to work, and helped by some other boys, he
made a rough model of a Marforio eight braccia
long, lying down, which astonished every one, not
so much at the work itself, as at the spirit with
which so small a boy set himself to so great a work.

His father seeing his inclination, put him under the
care of Rustici, the best sculptor of the city, with
whom Lionardo da Vinci had constant intercourse.
He saw Baccio's drawings and was pleased with
them, and praising to him Donatello's works, bade
him do something in marble.

At this time the cartoon of Michael Angelo in
the Council Hall was uncovered, and all the artists
ran to copy it, and Baccio among others. He went
more frequently than any one, having counterfeited
the key of the chamber. In the year 1512, Piero
Soderini was deposed and the house of Medici rein-
stated. In the tumult, therefore, Baccio, being by
himself, secretly cut the cartoon into several pieces.
Some said he did it that he might have a piece of
the cartoon always near him, and others that he
wanted to prevent other youths from making use of

it ; others again that he did it out of affection for Lionardo da Vinci, or from the hatred he bore to Michael Angelo. The loss anyhow to the city was no small one, and Baccio's fault very great.

Having obtained the name of a good draughtsman, he desired to learn how to paint in colours, being firmly of opinion that he should not only equal Buonarroti, but surpass him greatly, but he wished to pretend that he had found out how to manage the colours by himself and had not been taught by others. He went therefore to his friend Andrea del Sarto, and asked him to paint his portrait in oils, thinking he should get two things by this scheme ; first, he should see how the colours were mixed, and then the picture would be his and he could use it as a model. But Andrea perceived what Baccio was about, and was angry at his artfulness, although he would have been ready to show him all he wanted if he had asked him as a friend. However he did not pretend to have found him out, but instead of mixing his colours as he usually did, he put them all on to his palette at once, and mixed them together with his brush, taking a little now of one and now of another with great rapidity, so that Baccio, being obliged to sit still if he wanted to be painted, could not discover what he wished to know. Nevertheless Baccio did not give up his desire, but was assisted by the painter Il Rosso, whom he told more openly what he wanted. He also gave himself to the study

of anatomy, persevering in it for many months and
years.   And certainly there was in this man'a desire
of honour and of working well in his art which is
greatly to be praised.   He spared no fatigue and
wasted no time, but was always intent on his work.

When Leo X. passed through Florence and the
city was decorated in his honour, a colossal statue
was entrusted to Baccio.   It was a Hercules, and
from Baccio's talk it was expected to surpass Buonarroti's David, but as his deeds did not correspond
with his words, nor the work to his boasts, Baccio
lost greatly in the esteem of artists and of all the city.
Pope Leo then sent him to help Andrea Contucci in
some works that he was employed upon at Loreto.
And when he came there he was received gladly by
Andrea, and welcomed because of his fame and
because the Pope had recommended him.   A piece
of marble being assigned him he set to work, but
being a person who could not endure rivalry, and
seldom praised other people's work, he began to find
fault with Andrea's work to the other sculptors,
saying it was wanting in drawing, and he said the
same of the others, so that in a little while he had
aroused a great deal of ill-will.   Then what he had
said coming to Andrea's ears, he, like a wise man,
began to reprove him gently, saying that sculpture
was to be done with the hands and not with the
tongue, and that he ought to speak of him with more
respect.   But Baccio replied to him with such in-

sulting language that Andrea could bear it no longer, and rushed upon him as if to murder him, but some people coming in hindered him. So Baccio was forced to depart from Loreto and come to Rome.

Now about that time there came two ambassadors from King Francis, and they going to see the Belvedere statues, praised greatly the Laocoon. The Cardinals de' Medici and Bibbiena, who were with them, asked if the king would value such a thing, but they replied it would be too great a gift. Then the cardinal answered that either this statue, or one so like it that the difference could not be found out, should be sent to his Majesty. And he resolved to have a copy made of it, and remembering Baccio, he sent for him and asked if he had courage to make a Laocoon equal to the original. Baccio replied that not only would he make one equal to it, but he would surpass it in perfection. So the cardinal resolved it should be done, and while the marble was coming Baccio made a model in wax, and a cartoon in black and white of the same size as the statue. Then the marble arrived, and Baccio, having made a screen in the Belvedere, set to work. But before it was very far advanced the Pope died, and Adrian VI. being made in his room Baccio returned with the cardinal to Florence. But when Adrian was dead, and Clement VII. became pope, he returned to Rome and to his Laocoon, which he completed in two years with greater excellence than he had ever shown.

He also restored the right arm of the ancient statue which had been broken off and was never found. The work appeared so good to His Holiness that he changed his mind and determined to send some other ancient statues to the king, and to send this to Florence, where it was placed in the palace of the Medici.

Now in the time of Leo X., while the marble for the S. Lorenzo of Florence was being hewn in Carrara, another piece had been cut nine and a half braccia high and five broad. Michael Angelo had designed to carve from this Hercules killing Cacus, to be placed by the side of his colossal David, and had made many drawings for it; but the death of Leo had stopped everything. When Clement was made pope, however, he desired that Michael Angelo should resume his work on the tombs of the Medici heroes in S. Lorenzo, and it was necessary to get more marble. The expense of these works was under the care of Domenico Boninsegni. He tried secretly to persuade Michael Angelo to join him in defrauding the Pope, but Michael Angelo refusing, Domenico took such a hatred to him that he did everything he could to annoy him, but covertly. He persuaded the Pope to give the marble for the colossal statue to Baccio, who at that time had nothing to do, saying that his Holiness would be better served by stirring up two such great men to emulation. His counsel pleased the Pope, and he followed it. Baccio was

granted the marble, and made a wax model of the
Hercules. He was sent to Carrara to see the marble,
and orders were given that it should be brought by
water to Signa on the river Arno. But when it arrived
there, the river being low between Signa and Florence, they determined to take it by land, and while
being disembarked it fell into the water, and through
its great weight sank so deep in the mud that they
could not get it out. However the Pope commanded
that the marble was to be recovered by some means
or other, and at Piero Rosselli's suggestion they
turned the river out of its course, and by means of
cranes and levers brought it to land. The accident
tempted many to write Tuscan and Latin verses
satirizing Baccio, who was much hated. One of
them related how the marble, knowing the genius of
Buonarroti, and fearing to be disfigured by Baccio's
hands, had flung itself into the river in despair at
such a fate. While the marble was being brought to
land, Baccio measuring it found that he could not
cut out of it the statue he had modelled. Going
therefore to Rome he showed the Pope that he must
give up his first model and make another. Having
planned many, he at last made one that pleased the
Pope, and returning to Florence, he found that the
marble had been brought thither, and began therefore
to work upon it. But in the year 1527 the Medici
left Florence after the sack of Rome, and Baccio,
not feeling himself secure in consequence of a private

quarrel with a neighbour who was of the popular
faction, went away to Lucca. The popular party
thus ruling Florence, entrusted Michael Angelo with
the fortifications of the city, and showed him the
marble upon which Baccio had begun to work, proposing, if it were not too much spoilt, that he should
take it and make two figures after his own manner.
Michael Angelo considering it, determined to give up
the Hercules and make instead Samson with two
Philistines, having killed one of them, and being
about to slay the other with the jawbone of the ass.
But the war being directed against the city of
Florence, Michael Angelo had other things to think
about than polishing marble, and was obliged to
leave the city.

When the war was over Pope Clement made
Michael Angelo return to the sacristy of S. Lorenzo,
and sent Baccio back to his giant. He, to show himself affectionately attached to his Holiness, wrote to
him every week, not only about things of art, but
entering into particulars about the citizens and those
who administered the government. This behaviour
brought down upon him more hatred than ever, and
the citizens hindered his work as much as ever they
could. But when Pope Clement and the emperor
met at Bologna, Baccio went to kiss the Pope's feet,
and told him of the hindrances and annoyances to
which he was subjected, and being terrible with his
tongue, he persuaded the Pope to charge Duke Ales-

sandro to take care that the work was brought to a
conclusion. So he returned to Florence, and working
at it continually, at last finished it. Duke Alessandro,
in consequence of the ill-feeling of the citizens, did
not care to have it set up, but the Pope interceding, it
was with great labour brought to the piazza and set
in its place. It would not be easy to describe the
multitude that filled the piazza for two days coming
to see the giant directly he was uncovered ; and
many different opinions were given, but all blaming
the work and the sculptor. Tuscan and Latin
verses were affixed to the pedestal, but some of them
going beyond any reasonable limit, Duke Alessandro,
considering that the statue was a public work, was
forced to throw some of the writers into prison, which
stopped people's mouths. Baccio, considering his
work, thought that in the open air the muscles
seemed too weakly marked, so he set up a new
scaffold and deepened the markings. But by those
who are capable of judging, it has been always held
to be well studied, and the figure of Cacus specially
well managed. In truth Michael Angelo's David,
standing near it, and being the most beautiful colossal statue that ever was made, deprives it of much
of the praise it deserves ; but if one considers Baccio's
Hercules by itself, it cannot but receive great commendation.

Baccio, desiring to hear what people said of it, sent
an old pedagogue whom he kept in the house into the

piazza, bidding him report to him what he heard. He returned in quite a melancholy state to the house, having heard nothing but evil, and when Baccio questioned him, replied that all with one voice found fault with it and that it did not please them. "And you, what do you say of it?" said Baccio. "I speak well of it, and it pleases me." "I do not want it to please you," said Baccio; "speak evil of it too, for, as you may remember, I never speak well of anybody, so we are quits." So he dissembled his vexation and, according to his custom, pretended not to care that people found fault with his works. Nevertheless his disappointment was really great, for when men labour hard for honour and only earn blame, although the blame may be unjust, the heart is secretly distressed and tormented by it. He was consoled by the gift of an estate from Pope Clement, which was doubly dear to him because it was close by his villa of Pinzerimonte and had belonged to Rignadori the rebel, his mortal enemy.

After the death of Pope Clement he heard that the Cardinal Ippolito de' Medici, with three other of the cardinals and Baldassare Turini, were executors of his will, and that they were to appoint the sculptors who were to make the statues of Leo and Clement. The work had been promised to Alfonso Lombardi by Cardinal de' Medici, but as he was going to meet Charles V. he died of poison. As soon as Baccio heard this he set off for Rome, and went to Madonna

Lucrezia Salviata de' Medici, Pope Leo's sister, and
sought to show her that no one could do greater
honour to the memory of these pontiffs than himself,
and that Alfonso could not without the aid of others
accomplish such an undertaking. He worked also
by other means and in other ways, and succeeded in
making them change their minds and entrust the
statues and reliefs to him. He made therefore two
models, in which he showed either too little religion
or too much adulation, or perhaps both, and when
they were finished he took them to the garden of
Cardinal Ridolfi, where the other cardinals and Baldassare were assembled. While they were at dinner
Il Solosmeo a sculptor arrived, a bold, witty man, who
was fond of saying hard things of every one, and
who was no friend of Baccio's. A message came in
that Il Solosmeo was asking leave to enter. Ridolfi
bade them open to him, and then turning to Baccio
said, "I should like to know what Il Solosmeo says
about the monuments; lift the tapestry and go behind
it." Baccio obeyed, and when Il Solosmeo had come
in and they had given him something to drink, they
began upon the monuments that had been given to
Baccio to make. Il Solosmeo reproved the cardinals
for the bad choice they had made, and began saying
all kinds of evil of Baccio, accusing him of ignorance
in art and arrogance and avarice. Baccio, hidden
behind the tapestry, could not wait till Il Solosmeo
had done, but issuing forth in a rage cried out,

"What have I done to you that you speak of me with
so little respect?"   At the sight of Baccio Il Solosmeo became mute; then turning to Ridolfi he said,
"What deceivers these my lords are! I will have no
more to do with priests;" and he went away. But
the cardinals laughed heartily at both of them, and
Salviati turning to Baccio said, "You hear what is
the judgment of men of art; see to it that by your
work you give them the lie."

Nevertheless Baccio took little pains with the
work, and left it half finished; and having received
all the money, left Rome and went to Florence to
serve Duke Cosimo. And by little and little he grew
into such familiar favour with the duke that every
one feared him. He persuaded the duke to ask
Michael Angelo for some marbles that he had in
Florence, among which were some statues begun
and one more advanced, and when the duke had
obtained them and given them to Baccio, he cut
them to pieces and ground them to powder, thinking
thus to revenge himself and do despite to Michael
Angelo. Baccio made for the duke the ornaments
of his audience chamber, and many things for
S. Maria del Fiore.

In those days came Benvenuto Cellini from France,
having served the King Francis as a goldsmith,
and he made for the duke a statue of Perseus and
other things. But as the potter always envies the
potter, so the sculptor does the sculptor, and Baccio

could not endure the favours that were shown to
Benvenuto. He thought it was a strange thing that
a goldsmith should suddenly become a sculptor, and
one who was used to medals and little figures should
undertake colossal statues. Nor could Baccio conceal his opinion, but betrayed it to every one, and he
now found one ready to answer him ; for saying evil
things of Benvenuto in the presence of the duke,
Benvenuto, who was no less proud, gave him back
what he received. The duke took pleasure in hearing them, for there was wit and acuteness in their
satire, and he gave them free leave to say what they
liked before him, but not abroad. However, one day
Benvenuto, after many bitter things had been said,
came up threatening and menacing Baccio, saying,
" Prepare yourself for another world, for I will send
you out of this ; " to which Baccio replied, " Let me
know the day before, that I may confess and make
my will, and not die like a beast as you are." Upon
this the duke imposed silence upon them, fearing
some ill end to the matter.

After that came Giorgio Vasari to serve his Excel-
lency in many things, and Baccio thought the duke
had no more use for him because he employed others
and in his grief and displeasure he became so strange
and full of humours that no one could hold any
converse with him ; even his son Clemente suffered
many things from him, and went to Rome to escape
from him, where the same year he died, a great loss

to his father and to art, as Baccio found out when
he was dead. He had left behind him a half-finished
sculpture of the dead Christ supported by Nicode-
mus, and when Baccio heard that Michael Angelo
was working upon the same subject in Rome, intending to put it over his tomb in S. Maria Maggiore, he began to work upon his son's, and with the
aid of others finished it. Then he went through all
the principal churches in Florence seeking for a
place in which to make his own tomb. And having
by the intercession of the duchess, who was ever
his friend, obtained a place in the church of the
Servites, he removed thither the bones of his father.
But whether it were from disturbance of mind, or
from fatigue in moving the marble, he went to his
house ill, and growing every day worse, died at the
age of seventy-two, having been until then so robust
that he had never known sickness.

CHAPTER XXIII.

RUSTICI.

It is a wonderful thing that all those who studied in the school of the Medici garden, and were favourites of the magnificent Lorenzo, became excellent masters. It could not have happened if this true Mecænas of men of talent had not been a man of great judgment, able to recognize genius as well as to reward it. Giovan Francesco Rustici having distinguished himself there, was placed by Lorenzo with Andrea del Verrocchio, with whom was the rarely gifted youth, Lionardo da Vinci. And Lionardo's manner greatly pleasing Rustici, when Andrea went to work in Venice, he joined himself to him, serving him with loving submission. Being of a noble family, he had enough to live upon, and gave himself to art for his pleasure and from desire of honour. To have to work indeed, as many have to do, to supply the need of the day, is not good for men who should be working for glory and honour, for good works do not come without long consideration. Rustici used to say in his more mature years that you should first think over your subject, then make sketches, afterwards drawings, and then put them away for weeks and months without looking at them, then choosing the best, set to work upon them, which no cne can do who works for gain.

When the Medici family returned to Florence, Rustici made himself known to Cardinal Giovanni as one who had been favoured by his father Lorenzo, and was received by him with many caresses. But the ways of the court did not please him, being contrary to his nature, which was quiet and sincere, and not full of envy and ambition.

Having come into some reputation, the consuls of the Guild of the Merchants entrusted to him the making of three bronze figures for the door of S. Giovanni, the subject being S. John preaching, with a Levite and Pharisee beside him. The work was greatly to his taste, being for a place so celebrated and important. He would have nobody near him when he worked but Lionardo da Vinci, who, while he was making the mould, and in fact until the statues were cast, did not leave him, so that many said (but they did not really know), that Lionardo worked at them himself, or at least aided him with his counsel. While he was working upon them Rustici, not liking the annoyance of having to ask the consuls or their servants for money, sold a farm which he had outside Florence. But after all the expense and trouble, he was badly remunerated by the consuls and the citizens. For one of the Ridolfi, out of private spite, or perhaps because Rustici had not shown him enough honour, nor let him see the figures before they were finished, was always against him. And when his work was to be valued, Rustici, having called Michael Angelo Buonarroti to act for him, at the persuasion of Ridolfi, Baccio d'Agnolo was named for the other side. At this Rustici was much grieved, saying before them all that it was strange that a wood carver should have to value the labours of a statuary, and almost told the magistrates they were a herd of oxen, to which Ridolfi answered that Rustici was a proud, arrogant man. But what was worse, the work which was well worth two thousand crowns was only estimated at five hundred, and this was never entirely paid, but only four hundred, through the intercession of Cardinal Giulio de' Medici. Rustici therefore, almost in despair, resolved never to work for the public again, nor in any case where the matter would depend upon more than one man.

So he withdrew into private, and lived a solitary life, only working for pastime and not to be idle. He used to go and stroll about outside the city, taking off his long robe and carrying it over his shoulder, and once, finding it hot, he hid it in a wood among some bushes, and going on to the palace of the Salviati, stayed there two days before he

remembered it. Then sending one of his men to
seek for it, when he saw he had found it, he exclaimed, "The world is too good ; it will not last
long." He was a man of great kindness and very
good to the poor, and would never let any one
go away without assistance, but keeping his money
in a basket, whether he had little or much, he
gave to those who asked. A poor man therefore,
who often went to him for alms, seeing him always
go to the basket, said, not thinking to be heard,
"Oh, if I only had what is in that basket my difficulties would soon be over." Rustici heard him,
and looking at him fixedly said, "Come here, I will
content you," and he emptied the basket into a
corner of his cloak. Niccolò Buoni, a great friend
of his, managed all his matters for him, and gave
him so much money every week. There never was
a man who delighted more in animals. He had a
porcupine which was so tame that it went about
under the table like a dog, and used to rub itself
against people's legs and make them draw back very
quickly. He had an eagle, and a crow who could
say many things as clearly as a human being. He
also gave himself to necromancy, and by the things
he did caused great terror to his pupils and acquaintances. He had walled up a place like a fishpond,
and in this he kept a great many snakes and worms,
which could not get out, and he used to take great
pleasure in standing watching their mad gambols.

There used to assemble in his rooms a number of good fellows called the Company of the Saucepan, which was limited to twelve members, and each one of the twelve might bring four and no more to their suppers. And each one was bound to bring something to the supper made with skill and invention, and when he came he presented it to the master of the feast, who handed it on to any one he liked. One evening when Rustici was giving a supper to his Company of the Saucepan, he ordered that, instead of a table, a great kettle or saucepan should be made out of a wine vat, and they all sat inside it, and it was lighted from the handle which was over their heads. And when they were all comfortably settled, there rose up in the middle a tree with many branches bearing the supper, that is, the food on plates. And then it descended again and brought up a second course, and afterwards a third, and so on, while there were servants going round with precious wines and musicians playing below. This was greatly praised by the men of the Company. Rustici's dish that time was a cauldron made of pastry, in which Ulysses was dipping his father to make him young again. The two figures were capons with their limbs arranged to make them look like men. Andrea del Sarto, who was one of the Company, presented a temple with eight sides, like S. Giovanni, but resting on columns. The pavement was of gelatine, like different-coloured mosaics; the pillars, which looked like porphyry, were great sausages, the base and capitals of Parmesan cheese, the cornices of sugar, and the tribunes of marchpane. In the middle was placed the choir desk of cold veal, with a book of macaroni paste, having the letters and notes for singing made with peppercorns, and those who were singing were thrushes with their beaks open and wearing little surplices, and behind these for the bassi were two fat pigeons, with six ortolans for the soprani. Spillo, another member, brought the model of a smith, made of a great goose, or some such bird, with all the tools for mending the saucepan if it were necessary. Domenico Puligo brought a roast pig, made to represent a girl with her distaff by her side watching a brood of chickens. The other things represented were also very good, but we cannot tell them one by one.

There was also the Company of the Trowel to which Giovan Francesco belonged, and which began in this way. A supper was being given by Feo d'Agnolo, a humpbacked piper and a very amusing fellow, in his garden in the Campaccio, and while they were eating their *ricotta*, Il Baja, one of the guests, noticed a little heap of mortar, with a trowel lying by it, as a mason had left it the day before. Taking a little of the mortar on the trowel, he popped it into Feo's mouth, which happened to be opening for a great mouthful of *ricotta*, upon which all the company cried aloud, "A trowel! a trowel!" Out

of this incident the Company was formed, which was
to contain twenty-four members, the sign of which
was a trowel (*cazzuola*) to which they added those
little black vessels with a large body and a tail which
are also called *cazzuole.* Their patron saint was
S. Andrew, and they celebrated his feast day with a
solemn supper.

Before many years had passed it grew into such
reputation that Giuliano de' Medici and many other
important people joined it. Their feasts were in-
numerable. On one occasion, under the direction of
Bugiardino and Rustici, they all appeared in the
dress of masons and labourers, and set to work to
build an edifice for the Company with *ricotta* for
mortar, cheese for sand. The bricks, carried in
baskets and barrows, were loaves of bread and cakes.
But their building being pronounced badly done, it
was condemned to be pulled down, upon which they
threw themselves upon the materials and devoured
them all. At the end, when it was time to break up,
there came a cleverly managed shower of rain with
much thunder, which forced them to leave off work
and return home.

Another time Ceres seeking Proserpine came to
the members of the Company and prayed them to
accompany her to the lower regions. Descending,
they found Pluto, who refused to give her up, but
invited them to his wedding feast, where all the
provisions were in the form of horrid and disgusting

animals, snakes, spiders, frogs, and scorpions, and such creatures, which being opened contained food of the most delicate kinds.

Another time the master of the feast, intending to reprove some who had spent too much on the banquets of the Company, eating themselves alive, as the expression is, arranged his banquet in this way. At the place where they were used to meet, he caused to be painted on the façade such figures as are usually seen represented on the outside of an almshouse or hospital, the master receiving the poor and strangers, and this picture was uncovered just as the members arrived. They were received in a large room like the wards of a hospital, with beds on each side, and in the middle of the room near a great fire were some of the members dressed like beggars, who taking no notice of the others coming in, carried on a conversation about the Company and themselves, abusing them for throwing away more than was right in feasts and suppers. And when all the guests were come, S. Andrew, their patron, came in, and delivering them from the poor-house, led them to another room magnificently prepared, where they sat down to supper and feasted gaily, after which their saint commanded them to content themselves with one feast a year, and so save themselves from the poor-house. And this command they obeyed, having one magnificent feast only, with a dramatic representation.

But to return to the life of Rustici. After the Medici were driven out in 1528, not finding life at Florence to his taste, he went to France, and was received by King Francis with great favour, and received a provision of five hundred crowns a year. But when King Francis died and Henry began his reign, the expenses of the court being curtailed, his pension was taken from him, and he being now old, was reduced to living on the rent of a palace which Francis I. had given him. But fortune inflicted another blow upon him, for King Henry presented this palace to Signor Piero Strozzi, and Rustici found himself in extreme need. But Strozzi, hearing of his ill fortune, came to his aid and sent him to an abbey, or some such place, which belonged to his brother, where he was taken care of to the end of his life.

CHAPTER XXIV.

In the year 1523 Silvio Passerini, Cardinal of Cortona, passed through Arezzo, and Antonio Vasari, being a kinsman of his, went to pay his respects to him, taking his eldest son Giorgio with him. The cardinal finding that the child, who was only nine years old, had been already introduced to the study of letters, so that he knew a great part of Virgil by heart, and that he had learnt drawing from a French painter, desired that Antonio Vasari should take his child to Florence. There he placed him in the house of Niccolò Vespucci, a knight of Rhodes, who dwelt near the Ponte Vecchio, and sent him to study under Michael Angelo Buonarroti. At this time Francesco was living in the lane by Messer Bivigliano's house with his father, a velvet weaver, and as every creature loves its like, he made friends with Giorgio through M. Marco da Lodi, who showed Giorgio a portrait painted by this Francesco, who had just been placed with the painter Giuliano Bugiardini, which pleased him greatly.

Vasari had not then given up the study of letters, but by the cardinal's orders was working for two hours every day with Ippolito and Alessandro de' Medici, under their master Il Pierio. The friendship then contracted between Vasari and Francesco has always lasted between them, though from a certain haughty way of speaking which Francesco had, and from their competing against each other, some have thought otherwise. Vasari, having been some months with Michael Angelo, was placed by him with Andrea del Sarto when he had to go to Rome; and then Giorgio used secretly to convey his master's drawings to Francesco, who had no greater desire than to study them day and night. Afterwards also, when Giorgio was placed by the magnificent Ippolito with Baccio Bandinelli, who was glad to have the boy, he would not rest till he had got Francesco there too, to the great profit of both, for learning and working together, they made more progress in a month than they would have done otherwise in two years.

When the Medici were driven out in 1527, during the fighting round the palace of the Signoria, a bench was thrown down upon those who were fighting round the gate, but, as fortune would have it, it struck the arm of Buonarroti's David, and broke it into three pieces. And when the pieces had lain on the ground for three days without any one touching them, Francesco went to the Ponte Vecchio and sought out Giorgio, and the two boys together went to the piazza; and going among the soldiers on guard, without considering the danger, they picked up the pieces and carried them to the house of Francesco's father, where afterwards Duke Cosimo found them and had them repaired with copper rivets.

The Medici being thus banished, and with them the Cardinal of Cortona, Antonio Vasari took his son back to Arezzo, to the no small grief both of himself and of Francesco, for they loved each other like brothers. But they were not long separated, for the next August Giorgio lost his father and others of his family by the plague, and being urged by letters from Francesco, who had himself nearly died of it, he returned to Florence, and they worked together for two years with such incredible earnestness that they made marvellous progress. Afterwards Francesco went to be with Andrea del Sarto, and was there during the siege, suffering such hardships that he repented he had not gone with Giorgio, who was staying that year at Pisa.

Not long afterwards Benvenuto dalla Volpaia, the clockmaker, being in Rome, was asked by Cardinal Salviati to tell him of a young painter to live with him and paint for him, and Benvenuto proposed Francesco. The cardinal being pleased with his description of him, gave him money for his journey; and so Francesco went to Rome, where his manners pleasing the cardinal, he ordered that rooms should be given him and four crowns a month, and a place at his gentlemen's table. Francesco being in Rome, had no greater desire than to see his friend Giorgio Vasari in that city, and fortune was favourable to him, and still more to Vasari; for Cardinal Ippolito, passing through Arezzo, found Giorgio, who had lost his father and was getting on as best he could, and gave orders that he should go to Rome. As soon as Giorgio arrived there he went at once to Francesco, who told him joyfully in what high favour he was with the cardinal his master, and that he was in a place where he could satisfy every desire for study, adding, " I am not only enjoying myself now, but I hope for better things still, for besides having you here in Rome to talk with over matters of art, I am hoping to get into the service of Cardinal Ippolito de' Medici, from whose liberality and the favour of the Pope I may expect more than I have at present, and I shall be a made man, if a youth who is expected does not come." Giorgio knew that the youth who was expected was himself, and that the place was kept for him, but he would not say anything, thinking it possible that the cardinal might have some-one else in his mind. At length they went to the palace, and Giorgio was received kindly by the cardinal, and orders were given that rooms should be prepared for him, and a place at the page's table. Francesco thought it strange that Giorgio had not confided the matter to him, but concluded he had done it for good reasons, and all that winter they

studied together, leaving nothing noteworthy in Rome
which they did not draw. And because they could
not draw when the Pope was in the palace, as soon
as he had ridden forth to his villa of the Magliana,
they went into the rooms and stayed there from
morning to night without eating anything but a little
bread, and sometimes chilled with cold. But in the
July of the next year Giorgio, from the hardships of
the winter and the heat of the summer, fell ill and
was carried in a litter to Arezzo, to the great grief
of Francesco, who also was taken ill and nearly died.
He recovered however, and was entrusted with some
work in S. Maria della Pace, and considering that it
was not only for a public place, but also in a church
where were pictures by the greatest men, Raffaello
and others, he put his whole powers into the work,
and succeeded very well. As Francesco was living
with Cardinal Salviati, and was known as his depen-
dant, he began to be called Cecchino Salviati, which
name he bore till his death.

But in the year 1536 great and sumptuous prepara-
tions were made for the coming of Charles V., and
all the artists good and bad were employed under the
direction of Antonio da San Gallo. Francesco was
charged with some pictures in chiaroscuro, which
were placed on the Arch of San Marco, and which
were the best in the decorations. At the same time
there was painting there a Venetian, Battista Franco,
who had given much time to drawing, studying only

the drawings, pictures, and sculptures of Michael Angelo. If however he had learnt earlier to paint, and had studied the management of colours, he would have excelled. But remaining obstinately of the opinion, which many hold, that drawing is enough for a painter, he did himself great harm. When Salviati afterwards was employed by the Company of the Misericordia, Battista sought to be employed there also, thinking to show himself greater than Francesco, and the best master in Rome. But although he carried out the picture with great labour and pains, it was a long way from being equal to Salviati's, being in a crude melancholy manner, and without the grace and pleasant colouring that Francesco's had.

Afterwards entering the service of Duke Giudobaldo of Urbino, Battista was employed in making designs for the pottery works at Castel Durante, where they made great use of engravings from the works of Raffaello and others. This porcelain, as far as the quality of the clay goes, resembles much what used to be made in old days in Arezzo, in the time of Porsena, king of Tuscany. But the Romans had not this sort of painting on their vases, as far as we can tell. For the vases which are found from those days containing the ashes of the dead, and others besides, have figures outlined on one colour only, black or red or white, but never with a vitreous lustre, nor with those pleasant pictures which we see in our time. Nor can it be said that perhaps they had them, but that they have been destroyed by time or by being buried in the earth; for we see that ours can resist time and everything, and they might be buried for four thousand years under the ground and the pictures would not be spoilt. But although vases and painted china are made all over Italy, the best and most beautiful are those which are made at Castel Durante, a place in the State of Urbino, and those of Faenza, which are for the most part very white, with the design in the centre or round the border, very pleasantly and gracefully drawn.

But to return to Francesco Salviati. He was called upon now for many other pictures, which he showed Giorgio when he went to Rome for two months, after the death of Duke Alessandro. And he told him that when he had finished some pictures upon which he was employed he meant to return to Florence, that he might see his native city and his friends, for his father and mother were still living. He had always assisted them greatly, especially in settling his sisters, one of whom was married, and the other a nun in the convent of Monte Domini. He came therefore to Florence, and was received with great joy by his relatives and friends; and coming just at the time of the wedding of Duke Cosimo, one of the pictures to be painted for the occasion was entrusted to him. He

ITALIAN FAIENCE OF THE SIXTEENTH CENTURY.

undertook it gladly, but before it was finished went away to Venice, leaving it to another to complete. He was afterwards urged to return, as being certain to be employed by Duke Cosimo, who had no good masters round him ; so being persuaded, he came and obtained permission to paint a hall of the ducal palace, desiring no payment, but only leave to paint there. He put forth his utmost efforts in this work, desiring to leave a worthy memorial of himself in his native place. But he had many vexatious hindrances. For he was of a melancholy nature, and did not care to have people round him when he was working ; but at first, doing violence to his feelings, he allowed his friends to see him work. When however he found himself growing in favour with the court, he returned to his old choleric and satirical ways, and, what was worse, found fault with the works of others, and exalted his own to the skies. By this means he earned for himself such hatred that his former friends became his enemies, and did all they could to hinder him ; and by their malice and envy he was reduced to such a state that he wanted to leave the place altogether. His friends outside Florence, however, comforted him, and Giorgio Vasari, replying to a letter that Salviati wrote to him, desired him to have patience. So, in spite of all his persecutions, poor Francesco finished the hall, and produced other works for the duke.

In 1554 Andrea Tassini was charged to send a

painter to the King of France, and having asked Giorgio Vasari in vain (for he replied he would not leave the service of Duke Cosimo for any money), he agreed with Francesco. But before he left for France he sold all he had, thinking he should never return. But as soon as he arrived in Paris he was discovered to be a strange man, and, from whatever cause, his works were not much applauded. Neither was he himself much liked by the men of that country, for just as much as they like cheerful and jovial men who are fond of company and banquets, so are men like Francesco, who are melancholy, sober, and morose, I will not say avoided, but less loved and caressed. And although his constitution did not allow him to eat and drink too much, he might have been more pleasant in conversation. Finding the king therefore occupied in war, he determined to return to Italy, and coming to Florence, told Vasari he had done well in refusing to go to France, relating such things as would have checked any one's desire to go there. From Florence he went to Rome, and sought to have a share in the painting of the Hall of the Kings, which had been entrusted to Daniello da Volterra, and the matter was long in dispute between them, Michael Angelo favouring Daniello; but Vasari, loving the man, recommended him to Duke Cosimo, who did him so much service with the Pope that half the hall was entrusted to him. He set to work therefore, but first of all threw down a picture begun by Daniellò, and paid no attention to Pirro Ligorio the architect, who had been his friend. Pirro therefore, becoming in some sort his enemy, proposed to the Pope to employ many young men in the hall, which when Francesco heard and saw that the Pope was favourable to his proposal, he mounted his horse and rode away to Florence, where he established himself at an inn, as if he had had no friends and had not been a native of the place at all. Vasari therefore advised him to sell his things in Rome and settle at Florence. He however, moved by anger and the desire of revenge, returned to Rome ; but, afflicted in mind and of an unhealthy constitution, which he had weakened by constantly doctoring himself, he fell sick of a mortal disease, which brought him to his end.

CHAPTER XXV.

TITIAN.

TITIAN was born in the little town of Cadore, on the Piave, five miles from the Alps. He sprang from the family of the Vecelli, one of the most noble of those parts; and when he reached the age of ten years, showing a fine spirit and quickness of mind, he was sent to Venice to the house of one of his uncles, an honoured citizen. He seeing that the boy was much inclined to painting, put him with the famous painter Gian Bellino, under whose discipline he studied drawing, and showed himself in a short time to be endowed by nature with all that was necessary for the art of painting. Gian Bellino and the other painters of that country, having no knowledge of ancient art, were accustomed mostly, and in fact entirely, to draw from life, though in a dry, crude manner. Titian therefore learnt in this way. But when Giorgione da Castelfranco came, the manner of working did not altogether please him, and he began to give his works more softness and greater relief, following nature indeed, and imitating her as

well as he could in colour, but not making any drawing, holding firmly that painting in colours without
studying the drawing in a cartoon was the true and
best way of working. Titian then, seeing Giorgione's
method, left Gian Bellino's manner and adopted the
new way, imitating it so well that his pictures were
mistaken for works of Giorgione. And when Giorgione was employed upon the façade of the German
Exchange a part was given to Titian. Some gentlemen, not knowing that Giorgione had ceased to
work there, and that Titian was employed upon it,
meeting Giorgione one day, began to congratulate
him, saying he was doing better on this façade than
he had done on that one on the Grand Canal. And
this vexed Giorgione so much that until the work
was finished, and it was known that Titian had done
that part, he would not be seen, and from that time
he would not let Titian work with him or be his
friend.

In the year 1508 Titian published a woodcut of
his Triumph of the Faith. And I remember Fra
Sebastiano del Piombo talking to me about it, and
saying that if Titian had been to Rome, and had
seen Michael Angelo's work, and Raffaello's, and the
ancient statues, and had studied drawing, he would
have done astonishing things, because he had such a
fine method of colouring, and deserved the praise of
being the best imitator of nature in the matter of
colour of our time.

Giovanni Bellino having left unfinished at his
death the picture, in the hall of the Great Council, of
Frederic Barbarossa kneeling before Pope Alexander
III., Titian completed it, altering many things, and
introducing many portraits of his friends and others.
By this he obtained from the Signory an office which
is called the Senseria, which brings in three hundred
crowns a year. This office has usually been given to
the best painter of that city, with the duty of painting
from time to time their prince or Doge, at the price
of eight crowns only, paid them by this prince, and
this portrait is afterwards placed in his memory in
the palace of S. Mark's.

The Duke Alfonso of Ferrara having employed
Giovanni Bellino to paint a picture for a room in his
palace, he had been unable to complete it on account
of his age, and Titian therefore was summoned to
finish it, and for this prince he painted several things,
and was liberally rewarded by him. At this time
he formed a friendship with the divine Ludovico
Ariosto, who celebrated him in his "Orlando Fu-
rioso."

After his return to Venice he painted many pictures
for the churches, and among others for the church of
S. Rocco he painted Christ bearing the Cross. This,
which many have supposed to be from Giorgione's
hand, has become the chief object of devotion in
Venice, and has received in alms more crowns than
Titian and Giorgione earned in their whole life.

Bembo, who was then secretary to Pope Leo X., pressed him to come to see Rome, Raffaello, and others; but Titian went on putting it off from day to day until Leo and Raffaello both were dead.

When Pietro Aretino, before the sack of Rome, came to stay in Venice, he formed a great friendship with Titian, which was very useful to him, for he made him known as far as his pen could reach, and to princes of importance.

But to return to Titian's works. For the church of S. Giovanni and S. Paolo he painted an altarpiece representing S. Peter Martyr in a wood of high trees, struck down by a fierce soldier, who has wounded him in the head, and as he lies half alive you can see in his face the horror of death, while another friar fleeing shows signs of fear. In the sky are two angels coming in the light of heaven, which lights up a beautiful landscape. The work is the most finished one that Titian ever did.

When the Emperor Charles V. was in Bologna, Titian, at the suggestion of Pietro Aretino, was summoned by Cardinal Ippolito de' Medici to the palace, and painted a very fine portrait of his Majesty in full armour. Alfonso Lombardi had a great desire to portray him also, and having no other way of accomplishing it, he begged Titian to take him in the place of one of the men who carried the colours, not telling him what he was intending to do. Titian, like the courteous man he always

showed himself, agreed, and took him with him into
the emperor's room. Then, as soon as Titian had
set to work, Alfonso placed himself where he could
not be seen by him, and taking out a little box, he
modelled in gypsum a portrait medallion of the
emperor, and had just brought it to completion
when Titian had finished his portrait. When at
last the emperor rose, Alfonso closed the box, and
was hiding it in his sleeve that Titian might not see
it, when his Majesty said to him, "Show me what
you have done;" and he was obliged to put it into
his hand. The emperor having considered it and
praised it much, said, "Have you the courage to do
it in marble?" "Yes, your sacred Majesty," answered
Alfonso. "Do it then," replied the emperor, "and
bring it to me at Genoa." Any one can imagine how
strange this seemed to Titian. I fancy he thought
he had compromised himself. But what must have
seemed most strange to him was that his Majesty,
sending him one thousand crowns, bade him give half
to Alfonso and keep the other five hundred himself.
Alfonso, applying himself with the utmost diligence,
completed the head so successfully that it was pronounced a very rare piece of work, and when he
brought it to the emperor, his Majesty gave him
another three hundred crowns.

In the year 1546 he was called by Cardinal
Farnese to Rome, where he found Vasari employed
in the hall of the cardinal, and Titian being recom-

... completed the head so successfully that it was pronounced a very rare piece of work, and when it was brought in to the cardinal, his Eminence gave him another three hundred crowns.

In the year 1516 he was called by the Duke to Rome, where he found Vasari ... and ... of the cardinal, and Titian being too ...

THE DEATH OF PETER MARTYR. By TITIAN.

mended to his care, he took him about to see Rome. And after he had rested some days, rooms were given him in the Belvedere that he might paint the Pope Paul III., Cardinal Farnese, and Duke Ottavio, which he completed to their great satisfaction. Afterwards he painted an Ecce Homo to present to the Pope, but whatever the cause might be, it did not appear to painters equal to his other paintings, especially his portraits.

One day Michael Angelo and Vasari went together to see Titian in the Belvedere, and he showed them a picture he had just painted of Danaë in the shower of gold, and they praised it much. After they had left him, talking over Titian's work, Buonarroti commended him greatly, saying that his colour pleased him, but that it was a fault that at Venice they did not learn first of all to draw well, for if this man, he said, were assisted by art as he is by nature, especially in imitating life, it would not be possible to surpass him, for he has the finest talent and a very pleasant, vivacious manner.

Titian left Rome at length, having received many gifts, particularly a benefice with good revenues for his son Pomponio. Coming to Florence he saw the rare things in that city, and was no less astonished than he had been at Rome, and so returned to Venice.

But because his works are infinite, especially his portraits, it is impossible to mention them all. So

to speak only of the most remarkable without order
of time.   He painted Charles V. many times, and
was at last called to his court that he might paint
him as he was almost in his last years ; and so much
did he please that invincible emperor that he would
never afterwards be painted by any other painter,
and every time Titian painted him he had a donative
of one thousand crowns of gold.   His Majesty also
made him a knight, with a provision of two hundred
crowns from the treasury of Naples.   When he
painted the portraits of Philip King of Spain, and
his son Carlos, he received from him a settled provision of two hundred crowns ; so that, adding these
four hundred to the three hundred that he had from
the Venetian Signory, he received seven hundred
crowns a year without any labour for it.   He painted
Ferdinand King of the Romans, and his sons, and
the Queen Maria. But what is the use of losing time
in this way ?   There is no lord of note or prince or
great lady who has not been painted by Titian ; and
besides, at different times, he produced many other
works.

It is true that his way of working in his last
pictures is very different from that of his youth.
For his first works were finished with great diligence, and might be looked at near or far, but the
last are worked with great patches of colour, so that
they cannot be seen near, but at a distance they
look perfect. This is the reason that many think

they are done without any trouble, but this is not true. And this way of working is most judicious, for it makes the pictures seem living.

All these works, with a great many others, which cannot be mentioned lest I should become tedious, he has completed, having now reached the age of seventy-six. He has been most healthy, and as fortunate as any one has ever been. In his house at Venice he has received all the princes, and learned and famous men, who have come to Venice; for besides his excellence in art, his manners have been most pleasant and courteous. He has had some rivals, but not very dangerous ones. He has earned much, for his works have always been well paid; but it would be well for him, in these his last years, to work only for pastime, lest he diminish his reputation.

When the present writer was in Venice in 1566, he went to visit Titian, and found him, old as he was, with his brush in his hand painting, and he found great pleasure in seeing his works and talking with him.

Thus Titian having adorned Venice, or rather Italy, and other parts of the world, with the finest pictures, deserves to be loved and studied by artists, and in many things imitated, for he has done works worthy of infinite praise, which will last as long as illustrious men are remembered.

CHAPTER XXVI.

MICHAEL ANGELO.

IN 1474, under a lucky star, was born a son to Lodovico di Lionardo Buonarroti Simoni, descended, it is said, from the ancient and noble family of the Counts of Canossa. This Lodovico was Podestà that year of Chiusi and Caprese, near Vernia, where S. Francis received the stigmata, and, as I have said, there was born to him on Sunday the 6th of March, in the eighth hour of the night, a son, to whom he gave the name of Michael Angelo, perceiving that he was something greater than usual, Mercury and Venus at his birth being in the second house of Jove, which demonstrated that he would produce marvellous and stupendous works of art and genius. Lodovico, his time of office being finished, returned to Florence to Settignano, three miles from the city, where he had a small estate. The place was rich in a hard stone, which was constantly being worked by stonecutters, mostly born in the place, and the wife of one of these stonecutters was made nurse to Michael Angelo. Speaking of this once to Vasari, Michael Angelo said jestingly, " Giorgio, if I have anything of genius, it came to me from being born in the subtle air of your country of Arezzo, while from my nurse I got the chisel and hammer with which I make my figures."

As in time many sons were born to Lodovico, and his revenues were small, he set them to the woollen and silk trades, Michael Angelo, who was already growing up, being placed at school with Master Francesco da Urbino. But his inclination to the arts of design being strong, he spent all his time in drawing, as far as he could do so secretly, for he was often scolded by his father and those who were over him, and sometimes beaten for it, they supposing, perhaps, that it was a low thing, and unworthy of his ancient house. At that time Michael Angelo made friends with Francesco Granacci, who, being then a youth, had been placed with Domenico del Ghirlandajo to learn painting ; and Granacci loving Michael Angelo, and seeing him clever at drawing, used to give him every day drawings of Ghirlandajo's, who was esteemed not only in Florence but through all Italy as one of the best masters then living. By this means the desire grew stronger every day in Michael Angelo, and Lodovico, seeing there was no remedy for it, by the advice of his friends determined to put him with Ghirlandajo.

Michael Angelo was at this time fourteen years old, and he made such progress that he astonished

Domenico, who saw that he not only surpassed his other pupils, of whom he had a great number, but often equalled the things he did himself. It happened once that one of the boys who was learning there had copied with a pen some women out of one of Ghirlandajo's works, and Michael Angelo, taking the paper, with a thicker pen outlined one of the women again, as she should have been drawn ; and it is a wonderful thing to see the difference, and consider the courage of the youth who was daring enough to correct his master's things. I have this drawing still, as a relic, having received it from Granaccio ; and in the year 1550, when he was in Rome, Giorgio showed it to Michael Angelo, who recognized it and was glad to see it, saying modestly that he knew more of the art when he was a boy than now he was old.

At that time the magnificent Lorenzo de' Medici had filled his garden on the Piazza of S. Marco with ancient and good sculpture, so that the terraces and alleys were adorned with good antique figures in marble, and with pictures and other things by the best masters in Italy and elsewhere. And not only were they a great ornament to the garden, but they became a school and academy for young painters and sculptors, particularly for young nobles ; for Lorenzo held that those who are born of noble blood can more easily attain perfection in anything than those who come of low birth. Lorenzo therefore always favoured men of talent, but particularly nobles who had any inclination to art; so it is no wonder that some came forth from that school to astound the world. Besides this, he not only provided food and clothing for those who being poor could not afford time for study, but he also offered rewards for those who excelled in anything, that the youths by competing together might become more perfect. The head of this academy was Bertoldo, an an old Florentine sculptor and a pupil of Donatello's. He taught the youths, and at the same time had the care of the things in the garden, and the many drawings, cartoons, and models from the hand of Donatello, Brunellesco, Masaccio, Paolo Uccello, Fra Giovanni, and other masters native and foreign. And, indeed, these arts cannot be learned except by long study and by copying good works, and he who has not the opportunity, although he may be greatly endowed by nature, will be long in attaining perfection.

Lorenzo, therefore, lamenting that there were no great sculptors in his time, though there were many painters of the greatest fame, asked Domenico Ghirlandajo, if he had in his workshop any youths who were inclined to sculpture, to send them to his garden. Now Domenico held Michael Angelo and Francesco Granacci to be the best of his pupils. So these two going to the garden, found young Torrigiano there working upon some figures in clay as Bertoldo had directed him. This Torrigiano was by

nature very proud and choleric, and being robust
and fierce and courageous, he domineered over all
the others. His principal occupation was sculpture,
but he also worked in clay in a very beautiful
manner. He could not endure, however, that any
one should ever surpass him, and would with his
own hands injure any work of another which he could
not equal, and if the other resented it, they often
came to something more than words about it. He
took a particular dislike to Michael Angelo, for no
other reason than because he saw that he worked
studiously, and knew that he drew at home secretly
at night and on feast days, by which means he surpassed all the others in the garden, and was much
in favour with the great Lorenzo. Therefore, moved
by envy, he was always seeking to offend him in
word or deed, and having one day come to blows,
Torrigiano gave Michael Angelo such a blow with
his fist on his nose that he broke it, and Michael
Angelo bore the mark of it as long as he lived. The
thing having come to the ears of Lorenzo, he was
so angry that if Torrigiano had not fled from Florence
he would have been severely punished. He fled to
Rome, and was employed by Alexander VI. in the
building of the Borgia tower, but being led astray by
some Florentine youths, he turned soldier, and joining the Duke Valentino, bore himself valiantly in the
war in Romagna. He was afterwards in the war of
Pisa, and was with Pietro de' Medici in the deed of

arms on the Garigliano, where he obtained a pair of
colours and earned the name of the brave standard-
bearer. But finding he was never likely to attain to
the rank of captain, and had not advanced his own
affairs by war, but had rather lost his time, he
returned to sculpture. He made some little figures
in marble and bronze for some Florentine merchants,
and was by them brought to England. There he
worked for the king many things in marble, bronze,
and wood, competing with the masters of that land,
all of whom he surpassed; and he earned such
honours and rewards that if he had not been a person without any self-control, he would have lived and
died there quietly. However, leaving England, he
went to Spain, where he produced many works which
are much esteemed, and was charged by the Duke
of Arcos to make a Madonna and Child for him, the
duke making him such fine promises that he thought
he should be rich for ever. Having finished the
work, the duke paid him in those coins which are
called *maravedis,* which are worth little or nothing; but Torrigiano seeing two men loaded with
the money come to his house, was fully persuaded
that he was very rich. When, however, he had had
it counted by one of his Florentine friends, and
reduced to Italian money, he found there was not
quite thirty ducats. Upon this, supposing himself
to have been cheated, he went and destroyed in his
fury the statue he had made for the duke. The

Spaniard in his turn, considering himself insulted, accused Torrigiano of heresy. He was taken to prison, and brought up day after day, being sent from one inquisitor to another, and finally adjudged worthy of the gravest punishment. But meanwhile Torrigiano had fallen into a state of melancholy, and passed several days without eating, by which he brought himself to such weakness that he died, saving himself thus from shame, for it is said he had been condemned to death.

Another of the students in the garden of the Medici was Giuliano Bugiardini, who was united in close and intimate friendship with Michael Angelo, and loved him much. Michael Angelo returned his love, not because he saw anything very profound in him, but because he bore so much love to art. There was a certain natural goodness and simplicity in him without any envy or malice, which pleased Buonarroti infinitely. He had no other fault than loving his own works too much. But though this is a common fault with men, he passed all bounds; for which reason Michael Angelo used to call him blessed, because he was content with what he knew, and himself unhappy because his works never satisfied him fully.

Ottaviano de' Medici having secretly asked him to draw Michael Angelo, he set to work, and having kept him still for two hours, for he was fond of his conversation, he said to him, " Michael Angelo, if you would like to see yourself, come here, for I have just caught your look." Michael Angelo got up, and looking at the portrait said, "What have you done ? you have put one of my eyes in my temple ; look and see." Giuliano looked at it several times, and said, " It does not seem so to me ; but sit down and I shall see a little better how it is." Buonarroti, who saw what the mistake was, sat down laughing, and Giuliano looked again and again at Michael Angelo and the portrait, and then getting up at last said, " It seems that the thing is exactly as I have drawn it." " Then," answered Buonarroti, " it is a defect of nature ; go on, and do not spare pencils or art."

M. Palla Rucellai had given him a picture to paint for his altar in S. Maria Novella, and Giuliano began the martyrdom of S. Catherine, but he kept it on hand for twelve years, not having invention or knowledge enough for such a work. But Rucellai pressing for it to be done, he resolved one day to take Michael Angelo to see it, and having told him with what trouble he had made the lightning coming down from heaven and breaking the wheel, and the sun coming out of a cloud, he prayed Michael Angelo, who could not help laughing at his troubles, to tell him how to do eight or ten principal figures of the soldiers standing in a file on guard, for he could not see how to foreshorten them so that they should appear all in a row, or how he could find room for them in so narrow a place. Buonarroti, feeling compassion for the poor man, took up a piece of charcoal and sketched a file of naked figures with all the judgment and excellence proper to him, and went away with many thanks from Giuliano. Not long after, the latter brought Il Tribolo his friend to see what Buonarroti had done, and told him all about it; but because Buonarroti had only sketched them in outline, without any shadow, Bugiardini could not carry them out; so Il Tribolo resolved to help him, and he made some rough models in clay, giving them all that rough force which Michael Angelo had put into the drawing, and so he brought them to Giuliano. But this manner did not please Bugiardini's smooth fancy, and as soon as Il Tribolo was gone he took a brush and, dipping it in water, smoothed them all down. Il Tribolo, hearing about it from Giuliano himself, laughed at his honest simplicity, and the work was at last finished, so that none would have known that Michael Angelo had ever looked at it.

Giuliano, when he was old and poor, and doing little work, took great pains over a Pietà in a tabernacle which was to go to Spain. To represent the darkness at the death of the Saviour, he made a Night on a black ground, copying the figure from Michael Angelo's in the sacristy of S. Lorenzo. But that statue having no emblem but an owl, Giuliano added his own conceits—a net with a lantern for catching thrushes at night, a little vessel with a candle in it, besides nightcaps and pillows and bats. And when Michael Angelo saw the work he nearly killed himself with laughing at the strange things with which Bugiardini had enriched his Night.

Giuliano was once telling Il Bronzino how he had seen a very beautiful woman, and after he had praised her a great deal, Il Bronzino asked, " Do you know her ? " " No," he replied ; " but she is very beautiful. Think she is like a picture of mine, and that is enough."

But to return to Michael Angelo in the garden. When he saw Torrigiano's work in clay he was fired with emulation. He set himself to imitate an ancient head of an old faun, and although he had never touched marble or a chisel before, he succeeded so well that Lorenzo was quite astonished. Seeing that out of his own fancy he had opened the mouth and shown the tongue and teeth, De' Medici said in jest, but speaking gravely, as was his wont, " You ought to know that old men never have all their teeth, but have always lost some." Michael Angelo, with his simple respect and love for this lord, thought he spoke in earnest, and no sooner was he departed than he broke away a tooth and altered the gum to look as if he had lost it, and waited with desire the return of his Magnificence. He, when he came and saw the simplicity of Michael Angelo, laughed much, telling the story to his friends. But desiring to assist him, he sent for Lodovico his father,

and prayed to give him his son, and he would treat
him like a son of his own. And he willingly con-
senting, Lorenzo gave him a room in his house, and
he eat continually at his table with his sons and the
noble persons who were around his Magnificence.
This was in the year after he had gone to Domenico,
when he was about fifteen or sixteen years old, and
he stayed in that house four years, until the death
of the magnificent Lorenzo.

Afterwards Michael Angelo returned to his father's
house, but Piero de' Medici, Lorenzo's heir, often sent
for him, and one winter when it snowed heavily in
Florence, he made him make a statue of snow in his
courtyard, which was most beautiful. When the
Medici were driven out of Florence, Michael Angelo
was gone to Bologna and Venice, having left some
weeks before, for he feared some evil would befal him
from his intimacy with that house, seeing the inso-
lence and bad government of Piero de' Medici. He
tarried in Bologna a year and then returned to
Florence, where he made a sleeping Cupid, which
being shown by Baldassari del Milanese to Lorenzo
di Pier Francesco de' Medici, he said, " If you were
to bury it till it looked old, I am sure it would pass
for an antique, if you sent it to Rome, and you would
get much more for it than if you sold it here." Some
say that Michael Angelo did so, making it look old,
and others that Milanese carried it to Rome and
buried it in one of his vineyards, and then sold it as

an antique for two hundred ducats to the Cardinal S. Giorgio. However it may be, it brought such reputation to Michael Angelo that he was summoned to Rome by the Cardinal S. Giorgio, and tarried there a year, but the cardinal knowing little of art gave him nothing to do. Nevertheless during his stay in Rome he made much progress in the study of art, and the Cardinal de S. Denis, desiring to leave some worthy memorial of himself in so famous a city, caused him to make a Pietà in marble for the chapel of the Virgin in S. Peter's. To this work Michael Angelo bore such love that he inscribed his name on the girdle of our Lady, a thing he never did again. For one day Michael Angelo entering the place where it stood, found a number of Lombard strangers there. And as they were giving it great praise, one of them asked another who had made it, and he answered, " Our hunchback from Milan." Michael Angelo remained silent, but it seemed strange to him that his labours should be attributed to another. And one night he shut himself into the place with a light and cut his name upon it.

At this time some of his friends wrote to him advising him to come back to Florence, because there was some talk of having the great piece of marble which was lying spoilt, made into a statue, and Piero Soderini the Gonfaloniere had talked of giving it to Lionardo da Vinci, and now was preparing to give it to Andrea Contucci. Michael Angelo had desired to have it many years before; so he returned to Florence, and tried for it. It was a piece of marble nine braccia in size, out of which a master Simone da Fiesole had begun to carve a giant, and had managed it so badly that the heads of the works at S. Maria del Fiore, without caring to have it finished, had abandoned it, and it had been lying thus for many years. Michael Angelo measured it again, and examined it to see if a reasonable figure could be cut out of the rock by accommodating its attitude to the maimed condition in which Master Simone had left it, and resolved to make request for it from the architects and Soderini. They considering it a useless thing granted it to him, thinking that anything would be better than the state it was in. Then Michael Angelo made a model in wax of a young David with a sling in his hand, and began to work in S. Maria del Fiore, setting up a hoarding round the marble, and working at it continually without any seeing it until he had brought it to perfection. Master Simone had so spoilt the marble that in some places there was not enough left for Michael Angelo's purpose, and certainly it was a miracle restoring thus one that was dead.

When Piero Soderini saw it, it pleased him much, but he said to Michael Angelo, who was engaged in retouching it in certain places, that he thought the nose was too thick. Michael Angelo, perceiving that the Gonfaloniere was below the statue, and could not see it truly, to satisfy him went up the scaffold, taking a chisel in his left hand with a little marble dust, and began to work with his chisel, letting a little dust fall now and then, but not touching the nose. Then looking down to the Gonfaloniere, who was watching, he said, " Look at it now." " It pleases me better," said the Gonfaloniere; "you have given it life." So Michael Angelo came down pity-ing those who make a show of understanding matters about which they really know nothing. Michael Angelo received from Soderini for the statue four hundred crowns, and it was set up in the year 1504.

Lionardo da Vinci was now occupied in paint-ing the great Council Hall, and Pietro Soderini assigned one part of it to Michael Angelo, who chose for his subject the war of Pisa. He took a room in the dyers' hospital at S. Onofrio, and began a great cartoon, which he would not allow any one to see. He covered it with nude figures of the soldiers bathing in the river Arno and suddenly called to arms, the enemy making an assault. Some are coming out of the water, others are hastening to arm themselves and go to the help of their com-panions, buckling on their cuirasses and their other arms. When it was shown, many said that such a thing had never been seen before, either from his hand or another's. And indeed this is to be believed true, for all who have studied this cartoon have become men excellent in the art. And because it became thus a study for artists it was carried to the

Medici palace, and was left in too great security in the hands of the artists. For during the sickness of Duke Giuliano, when no one was thinking of the matter, it was torn and cut into many pieces, and dispersed in many places, some pieces being to be seen now in Mantua.

Michael Angelo's fame was grown so great that in the year 1503, when he was twenty-nine years of age, Julius II. sent for him to come and build his tomb. Therefore proceeding to Rome, after many months he resolved upon a design which in beauty, ornament, and the number of the statues surpassed every ancient or imperial sepulchre. Thereupon Pope Julius enlarged his projects, and resolved to rebuild the church of S. Peter's that it might contain it. So Michael Angelo set to work and went to Carrara with two of his youths to obtain the marble, and spent in those mountains eight months. Having chosen a quantity of marble, he caused it to be carried to the sea and thence to Rome, where it filled half the Piazza of S. Peter's, and round S. Caterina, and the space between the church and the corridor that goes to the castle, where Michael Angelo had made a room in which to work at the statues and the rest of the tomb. And that the Pope might easily come and see the work, he had a drawbridge made from the corridor to the room. Being treated with such familiarity he became exposed to great persecution, and much envy was aroused among the artists.

Of this work Michael Angelo finished four statues and began eight more. Some of the marble was carried to Florence, where he worked some time to escape the bad air of Rome. In Rome he made two Captives, and the Moses, which no other modern work will ever equal in beauty. Meanwhile the rest of the marble, which had been left at Carrara, arrived, and was carried to the piazza of S. Peter's, and it being necessary to pay those who had brought it, Michael Angelo went as usual to the Pope, but finding that his Holiness had important business in the affairs of Bologna, he returned home and paid for the marble himself. He returned another day to speak of it to the Pope, but found difficulty in obtaining admission, one of the lacqueys bidding him have patience, for he had orders not to let him in. A bishop said to the lacquey, "Perhaps you do not know this man;" but he answered, "I know him too well, but I am here to do what my superiors and the Pope command me." This displeased Michael Angelo, and thinking it treatment contrary to what he had before experienced, he replied in anger to the Pope's lacquey, bidding him say, when his Holiness asked for him, that he had gone elsewhere. He returned home and set off in haste at two o'clock of the night, leaving two servants with orders to sell all the things in the house to the Jews, and to follow him to Florence. He journeyed on till he reached Poggibonsi, a place in the Florentine

district.   It was not long before five couriers arrived
with letters from the Pope to bring him back; but
he would listen neither to their prayers nor to the
letters, which commanded him to return to Rome
under pain of disgrace. At last the couriers' entreaties
induced him to write a few words to his Holiness,
saying that he must pardon him for not returning
to his presence since he had been driven away,
that his faithful service had not deserved such treatment, and therefore his Holiness must seek elsewhere for one to serve him.   And so coming to
Florence he set himself to finish the cartoon for the
Great Hall, which Pier Soderini greatly desired he
should execute.   In the meantime there came three
briefs to the Signory, commanding them to send
back Michael Angelo to Rome.   He, perceiving the
fury of the Pope, meditated going to Constantinople
to serve the Turk, who desired to have him to con-
struct a bridge from Constantinople to Pera.   At
last Pier Soderini persuaded him against his will to
go back to the Pope, sending him back as a public
person, with the title of ambassador of the city, and
recommending him to his brother, Cardinal Soderini.
So he came to Bologna, whither his Holiness had
come from Rome.

Some tell the story of his departure from Rome in
another manner, and say that the Pope was angry
with Michael Angelo because he would not let him
see his work, and that he came more than once dis-

guised when Michael Angelo was not at home, and corrupted his lads with money to let him in to see the chapel of Sixtus his uncle, which he was painting, and that once Michael Angelo, doubting his boys, hid himself and let something fall upon the Pope as he entered the chapel, which made him rush out in a fury.

However it was, as soon as he reached Bologna, before he had taken off his boots, he was conducted by the Pope's servant to his Holiness, accompanied by a bishop from Cardinal Soderini, the cardinal himself being ill. Arrived in the Pope's presence, Michael Angelo knelt down, and his Holiness looked at him severely as if in anger, saying, "Instead of coming to us, you have waited for us to come to you," meaning that Bologna was nearer to Florence than Rome. Michael Angelo humbly begged pardon, saying he had not done it to offend, but that he could not endure to be driven away in such a manner. And the bishop who had brought him in began to excuse him, saying that such men were ignorant, except in matters of art, and were not like other men. Upon this the Pope grew angry, and with a stick he had in his hand he struck the bishop, saying, "It is you who are ignorant and speak evil of him, which we did not do." So the bishop was driven out from his presence by the lacquey, and the Pope having vented his anger upon him, blessed Michael Angelo, and showered upon him gifts and promises.

He was employed to make a bronze statue of Pope Julius, five braccia high, for the city of Bologna. The attitude is most beautiful, having great dignity, and in the drapery there is richness and magnificence, and in the countenance vivacity and force, promptness and terrible majesty. It was set up in a niche over the gate of St. Petronio. It is said that while Michael Angelo was working upon it, Francia the goldsmith and most excellent painter came to see it, having heard much of him and his works, and never having seen any of them. Gazing upon the work with astonishment, he was asked by Michael Angelo what he thought of it, and he answered that it was a very beautiful cast and a fine material. Michael Angelo, thinking that he was praising the bronze rather than the artist, said, " I am as much obliged to Pope Julius who gave it to me as you are to the men from whom you get your colours for painting," adding before some gentlemen that he was a fool.

Michael Angelo finished this statue in clay before the Pope left Bologna for Rome, and his Holiness went to see it. He asked what was to be in his left hand, and whether the right hand, which was raised with so haughty a gesture, was blessing or cursing. Michael Angelo replied that he was advising the people of Bologna to conduct themselves well, and prayed him to decide if he should put a book in his left hand, but he answered, " Put a sword, for I do not know letters." This statue was afterwards de-

stroyed by Bentivogli, and the bronze sold to Duke
Alfonso of Ferrara, who made it into a cannon called
the Julia, but the head is still preserved.

When the Pope was returned to Rome, Bramante
(a friend of Raffaello's, and therefore little a friend to
Michael Angelo) tried to turn his mind from finishing
his sepulchre, saying it was an evil augury and seemed
like hastening his death to make his own grave ; and
he persuaded him that on Michael Angelo's return
he should set him to paint the ceiling of the chapel
in the palace, in memory of Sixtus his uncle. For
Bramante and Michael Angelo's other rivals thought
to draw him away from sculpture, in which they saw
he was perfect, and make him produce less worthy
works, not to be compared with Raffaello's, knowing
he had had no experience in painting in fresco. So
when he was returned and proposed to the Pope to
finish his tomb, he desired him instead to paint the
ceiling of the chapel. Michael Angelo sought in every
way to shift the load off his back, proposing Raffaello
instead. But the more he excused himself, the more
impetuous the Pope became. So seeing that his
Holiness persevered, he resolved to do it, and the
Pope ordered Bramante to make the scaffold. He
made it hanging by ropes passed through holes in
the ceiling, which when Michael Angelo saw, he asked
Bramante how the holes were to be stopped up when
the painting was finished. He answered, " We must
think of that afterwards, but there is no other way."

So Michael Angelo knew that either Bramante was worth little or that he was no friend to him, and he went to the Pope and told him the scaffolding would not do. So he told him to do it his own way. He therefore ordered it to be made on supports, not touching the wall, and he gave to a poor carpenter who made it, so many of the useless ropes that by the sale of them he obtained a dowry for one of his daughters.

The Pope having resolved that the pictures which had been painted there by the masters before him in the time of Sixtus should be destroyed, Michael Angelo was forced by the greatness of the undertaking to ask aid and sent to Florence for men. And having begun and finished the cartoons, and never having coloured before in fresco, he brought from Florence some of his friends to aid him, and that he might see their method of working in fresco, among whom were Granacci, Bugiardini, and others. So he set them to begin the work, but their efforts being far from satisfying him, one morning he resolved to destroy all that they had done, and shutting himself up in the chapel, would not open the door for them, nor show himself to them at home. They therefore, after this had gone on some time, were offended, and took leave and went back to Florence with shame. Then Michael Angelo prepared to do the whole work himself, and brought it to a successful termination with great labour and study, nor would

he let any one see it, by which means the desire grew
strong in all. When the half was done and uncovered, all Rome went to see it, the Pope the first;
and Raffaello da Urbino, who was excellent in imitating, having seen it, changed his manner. Then
Bramante sought to persuade the Pope to give the
other half to Raffaello. But the Pope, seeing every
day the powers of Michael Angelo, judged that he
should finish the other half. So he brought it to an
end in twenty months by himself without even the help
of a man to grind the colours. Michael Angelo complained that from the haste of the Pope he could not
finish it as he would, for the Pope constantly asked
him when it would be finished. Once he answered,
" It will be finished when I have satisfied myself."
" But we will," replied the Pope, " that you should
satisfy us in our desire to have it quickly." And he
added that if it was not done soon he would have him
thrown from his scaffold. The Pope used often to
tell Michael Angelo to make the chapel rich in colour
and gold, but Michael Angelo would answer the Holy
Father, " In those times men did not wear gold, and
those whom I am painting were never very rich, but
holy men despising riches."

The work was done in great discomfort from constantly looking up, and it so injured his sight that he
could only read or look at drawings in the same position, an effect which lasted many months. But
in the ardour of labour he felt no fatigue and cared

for no discomfort. The work has been, indeed, a light of our art, illuminating the world which had been so many centuries in darkness. Oh, truly happy age, and oh, blessed artists, who at such a fountain can purge away the dark films from your eyes! Give thanks to heaven, and imitate Michael Angelo in all things.

So when it was uncovered every one from every part ran to see it, and gazed in silent astonishment; and the Pope inspired by it and encouraged to greater undertakings, rewarded him liberally with money and rich gifts. The great favours that the Pope showed him proved that he recognized his talents, and if sometimes he did him an injury, he healed it with gifts and signal favours; as when, for instance, Michael Angelo once asked leave of him to go to work in S. Giovanni in Florence, and requested money for the purpose, and he said, " Well, and this chapel, when will it be finished ? " " When I can, Holy Father." The Pope having a stick in his hand struck Michael Angelo, saying, "When I can! when I can! I will make you finish it!" Michael Angelo therefore returned to his house and prepared to leave for Florence, but the Pope in haste sent his chamberlain after him with five hundred crowns to pacify him, and ordered him to make his excuses and say it was all done in love and kindness. And he, seeing it was the nature of the Pope and really loving him, took it in good part and laughed at it, finding also that it turned to his profit, for the Pope would do anything to keep him his friend.

But when the chapel was finished, and before the Pope died, he gave orders to Cardinal Santiquattro and Cardinal Aginense, his nephew, that in the case of his death they were to complete his monument; but after a less magnificent design than the first. So Michael Angelo returned again to his work upon the tomb, hoping to carry it out to the end without hindrance, but it was to him the cause of more annoyance and trouble than anything else he did in his life. At that time befel the death of Julius, and the whole plan was abandoned upon the creation of Pope Leo X. For he having a mind and talents no less splendid than those of Julius, desired to leave in his native city, of which he was the first pontiff, such a marvellous work in memory of himself and of the divine artist, his fellow-citizen, as a great prince like himself was able to produce. So he gave orders that the façade of S. Lorenzo in Florence, a church built by the house of Medici, should be erected, and he commanded that the sepulchre of Julius should be abandoned that Michael Angelo might prepare plans and designs for this work. Michael Angelo made all the resistance he could, alleging that he was bound to Santiquattro and Aginense for the tomb. But the Pope replied that he was not to think about that, for he had already considered that, and had procured their consent to his departure. So the matter was settled to the displeasure both of the cardinals and Michael Angelo, and he departed weeping. He consumed many years in procuring marble, though in the meantime he made models in wax and other things for the work; but the matter was so delayed that the money set apart for it was consumed in the war of Lombardy, and the work was left unfinished at the death of Leo.

At this time, in the year 1525, Giorgio Vasari was brought as a boy to Florence by the Cardinal of Cortona and put with Michael Angelo to learn the art. But he being called by Pope Clement VII. to Rome, determined that Vasari should go to Andrea del Sarto, and went himself to Andrea's workshop to recommend him to his care.

When Clement VII. was made pope he sent for Michael Angelo, and he agreed with the Pope to finish the sacristy and library of S. Lorenzo, and to make four tombs for the bodies of the fathers of the two Popes, Lorenzo and Giuliano, his brother, and for Giuliano, brother of Leo, and Duke Lorenzo, his nephew. At this time befel the sack of Rome and the banishment of the Medici from Florence. Those who governed the city desired to refortify it, and made Michael Angelo commissary-general of all the fortifications. He surrounded the hill of S. Miniato with bastions and fortified the city in many places, and was sent to Ferrara to view the fortifications of Duke Alfonso, who received him with much courtesy, and prayed him at his leisure to make some work of art for him. Returning to Florence, and engaged again upon the fortifications, he nevertheless found time to make a painting of Leda in tempera for the duke, and to work upon the statues for the monument in S. Lorenzo. Of this monument, partly finished, there are seven statues, the first is our Lady, and though it is not finished, the excellence of the work may be seen. Then there are the four statues of Night and Day, Dawn and Twilight, most beautiful and sufficient of themselves if art were lost to restore it to light. The other statues are the two armed captains, the one the pensive Duke Lorenzo, and the other the proud Duke Giuliano.

Meanwhile the siege of Florence began, and the enemy closing round the city, and the hope of aid failing, Michael Angelo determined to leave Florence and go to Venice. So he departed secretly without any one knowing of it, taking with him Antonio Mini his pupil, and his faithful friend Piloto the goldsmith, wearing each one their money in their quilted doublets. And they came to Ferrara and rested there. And it happened because of the war that Duke Alfonso had given orders that the names of those who were at the inns and of all strangers should be brought him every day. So it came about that Michael Angelo's coming was made known to the duke. And he sent some of the chief men of his court to bring him to the palace, with his horses and all he had, and give him good lodging. So Michael Angelo, finding himself in the power of another, was forced to obey and went to the duke. And the duke received him with great honour, and making him rich gifts, desired him to tarry in Ferrara. But he would not remain, though the duke, praying him not to depart while the war lasted, offered him all in his power. Then Michael Angelo, not willing to be outdone in courtesy, thanked him much, and turning to his two companions, said that he had brought to Ferrara twelve thousand crowns and that they were quite at his service.

And the duke took him through his palace and showed him all his treasures, especially his portrait by the hand of Titian, which Michael Angelo commended much; but he would not stop at the palace, and returned to the inn, and the host where he lodged received from the duke an infinite number of things with which to do him honour, and command to take nothing from him for his lodging.

He proceeded thence to Venice, but many desiring to make his acquaintance, for which he had no wish, he departed from the Giudecca where he had lodged. It is said that he made a design for the bridge of the Rialto at the request of the Doge Gritti, a design most rare for invention and ornament.

But Michael Angelo was recalled by his native city, and earnestly implored not to abandon her, and

they sent him a safe conduct. At last, overcome by
his love for her, he returned, not without peril of his
life. He restored the tower of S. Miniato, which
did much injury to the enemy, so they battered it
with great cannon, and would have overthrown it,
but Michael Angelo defended it, hanging bales of
wool and mattrasses to shield it.

When the peace was made, Baccio Valore was
commissioned by the Pope to seize some of the
leading partisans, and they sought for Michael Angelo, but he had fled secretly to the house of a
friend, where he lay hid many days. When his
anger was passed, Pope Clement remembered his
great worth, and bade them seek him, ordering them
to say nothing to him, but that he should have his
usual provision and should go on with his work at
S. Lorenzo.

Then Duke Alfonso of Ferrara, having heard that
he had completed a rare piece of work for him, sent
one of his gentlemen to him that he might not lose
such a jewel, and he came to Florence and presented
his letters of credence. Then Michael Angelo showed
him the Leda, and Castor and Pollux coming out of
the egg ; but the messenger of the duke thought he
ought to have produced some great work, not understanding the skill and excellence of the thing, and he
said to Michael Angelo, " Oh, this is a little thing."
Then Michael Angelo asked him what was his trade,
for he knew that none are such good judges of a

thing as those who have some skill in it themselves. He replied contemptuously, " I am a merchant," thinking that Michael Angelo did not know he was a gentleman, and so being rather offended by the question he expressed some contempt for the industry of the Florentines. Michael Angelo, who perfectly understood his meaning, answered, " You have shown yourself a bad merchant this time, and to your master's damage; take yourself off." And afterwards, Anton Mini, his pupil, having two sisters about to be married, asked him for the picture, and he gave it to him willingly, together with the greater part of his drawings and cartoons, and also two chests of models. And when Mini went into France he took them with him there, and the Leda he sold to King Francis, but the cartoons and drawings were lost, for he dying in a short time they were stolen.

Afterwards the Pope desired him to come to him in Rome and paint the walls of the Sistine Chapel, and Clement wished that he should paint the Last Judgment and Lucifer driven out of heaven for his pride, for which many years before Michael Angelo had made sketches and designs. However, in 1533 followed the death of Pope Clement, and Michael Angelo again thought himself free to finish the tomb of Julius II. But when Paul III. was made pope, it was not long before he sent for him, and desired him to come into his service. Then Michael Angelo refused, saying he was bound by contract to the Duke of Urbino to finish the tomb of Julius II. But the Pope in anger cried out, " I have desired this for thirty years, and now that I am Pope I will not give it up. I will destroy the contract, and am determined that you shall serve me." Michael Angelo thought of departing from Rome, but fearing the greatness of the Pope, and seeing him so old, thought to satisfy him with words. And the Pope came one day to his house with ten cardinals, and desired to see all the statues for the tomb of Julius, and they appeared to him miraculous, particularly the Moses; and the Cardinal of Mantua said this figure alone was enough to do honour to Pope Julius. And when he saw the cartoons and drawings for the chapel, the Pope urged him again to come into his service, promising to order matters so that the Duke of Urbino should be contented with three statues, the others being made from his designs by good masters. The new contract, therefore, being confirmed by the duke, the work was completed and set up, a most excellent work, but very far from the first design; and Michael Angelo, since he could do no other, resolved to serve Pope Paul, who desired him to carry out the commands of Clement without altering anything. When Michael Angelo had completed about three-quarters of the work, Pope Paul went to see it, and Messer Biagio da Cesena, the master of the ceremonies, was with him, and when he was asked what he thought of it, he answered that he thought it

not right to have so many naked figures in the
Pope's chapel. This displeased Michael Angelo,
and to revenge himself, as soon as he was departed,
he painted him in the character of Minos with a
great serpent twisted round his legs. Nor did
Messer Biagio's entreaties either to the Pope or to
Michael Angelo himself, avail to persuade him to
take it away. At this time it happened that the
master fell from the scaffold, from no little height,
and hurt one of his legs, but would not be doctored
for it. Thereupon Master Baccio Rontini, the
Florentine, his friend and a clever doctor, having
pity on him, went one day and knocked at his door,
and receiving no answer, made his way to the room
of Michael Angelo, who had been given over, and
would not leave him until he was cured. When he
was healed, returning to his painting, he worked at
it continually, until in a few months it was brought
to an end, and the words of Dante verified, "The
dead seem dead and the living living." And when
this Last Judgment was uncovered, he was seen
to have vanquished not only all the painters who
had worked there before, but even to have surpassed
his own work on the ceiling. He laboured at this
work eight years, and uncovered it in the year
1541, on Christmas Day, I think, to the marvel of
all Rome, or rather all the world ; and I who went
that year to Rome was astounded.

Afterwards he painted for Pope Paul the Conver-

sion of S. Paul and the Crucifixion of S. Peter.
These were the last pictures he painted, at the age
of seventy-five, and with great fatigue, as he told
me ; for painting, and especially working in fresco,
is not an art for old men. But his spirit could not
remain without doing something, and since he could
not paint, he set to work upon a piece of marble, to
bring out of it four figures larger than life, for his
amusement and pastime, and as he said, because
working with the hammer kept him healthy in
body. It represented the dead Christ, and was left
unfinished, although he had intended it to be placed
over his grave.

It happened in 1546 that Antonio de Sangallo
died, and one being wanted in his place to order
the building of S. Peter's, his Holiness sent for
Michael Angelo and desired to put him in the office,
but he refused, saying that architecture was not his
proper art. Finally, entreaties availing nothing, the
Pope commanded him to accept it, and so, to his
great displeasure and against his will, he was obliged
to enter upon this office. Then one day going
to S. Peter's to see the model of wood which
Sangallo had made, he found the whole Sangallo
party there. They coming up to him said they
were glad that the charge of the work was to be
his, adding that the model was a field which would
never fail to provide pasture. " You say the truth,"
answered Michael Angelo, meaning to infer, as he

20

told a friend, "for sheep and oxen, who do not understand art." And he used to say publicly that Sangallo held more to the German manner than to the good antique, and besides that fifty years' labour might be spared and 300,000 crowns' expense, and yet the building might be carried out with more grandeur and majesty. And he showed what he meant in a model which made every one acknowledge his words to be true. This model cost him twenty-five crowns, and was made in fifteen days. Sangallo's model cost more than four thousand, it is said, and took many years to make, for he seemed to think that this building was a way of making money, to be carried on with no intention of its being finished. This seemed to Michael Angelo dishonest, and when the Pope was urging him to become the architect, he said one day openly to all those connected with the building, that they had better do everything to prevent him having the care of it, for he would have none of them in the building; but these words, as may be supposed, did him much harm, and made him many enemies, who were always seeking to hinder him. But at last the Pope issued his commands, and created him the head of the building with all authority. Then Michael Angelo, seeing the Pope's trust in him, desired that it should be put into the agreement that he served for the love of God and without any reward. But when a new Pope was made, the set that was opposed to him in Rome began again to trouble him, therefore the Duke Cosimo desired that he should leave Rome and return to Florence; but he being sick and infirm could not travel. At that time Paul IV. thought to have the Last Judgment amended, which when Michael Angelo heard he bade them tell the Pope that this was a little matter, and might easily be amended; let him amend the world, and then the pictures would soon amend themselves.

The same year befel the death of Urbino his servant, or rather, to speak more truly, his companion. He had come to him in Florence after the siege in 1530, and during twenty-six years served him with such faithfulness that Michael Angelo made him rich, and loved him so much that when he was ill he nursed him and lay all night in his clothes to watch him. After he was dead, Vasari wrote to him to comfort him, and he replied in these words :—

"My dear Messer Giorgio,—It is hard for me to write; nevertheless, in reply to your letter, I will say something. You know that Urbino is dead, to my great loss and infinite grief, but in the great mercy of God. The mercy is that dying he has taught me how to die, not in sorrow, but with desire of death. I have had him twenty-six years, and have found him most rare and faithful; and now that I had made him rich, and hoped that he would have been the support of my old age, he has left me, and nothing remains but the hope of meeting him again in paradise. And of this God gave me promise in the happy death he died, for he regretted, far more than death, leaving me in this treacherous world with so many infirmities, although the chief part of me is gone with him, and nothing remains but infinite misery."

Until this time Michael Angelo worked almost every day at that stone of which we have spoken before, with the four figures, but now he broke it, either because the stone was hard or because his judgment was now so ripe that nothing he did contented him. His finished statues were chiefly made in his youth ; most of the others were left unfinished, for if he discovered a mistake, however small, he gave up the work and applied himself to another piece of marble. He often said this was the reason why he had finished so few statues and pictures. This Pietà, broken as it was, he gave to Francesco Bandini. Tiberio Calcagni, the Florentine sculptor, had become a great friend of Michael Angelo's through Bandini, and being one day in Michael Angelo's house, and seeing this Pietà broken, he asked him why he had broken it, and spoilt so much marvellous work. He answered it was because of his servant Urbino's importunity, who was always urging him to finish it, and besides that, among other things, he had broken a piece off the Virgin's arm, and before that he had taken a dislike to it, having many misfortunes because of a crack there was in it; so at last losing patience he had broken it, and would have destroyed it altogether if his servant Antonio had not begged him to give it him as it was. Then Tiberio spoke to Bandini about it, for Bandini desired to have a work of Michael Angelo's, and he prayed Michael Angelo to allow Tiberio to finish it for him, promising that Antonio should have two hundred crowns of gold, and he being content, made them a present of it. So Tiberio took it away and joined it together, but it was left unfinished at his death. However, it was necessary for Michael Angelo to get another piece of marble, that he might do a little carving every day.

The architect Pirro Ligorio had entered the service of Paul IV., and was the cause of renewed vexation to Michael Angelo, for he went about everywhere saying that he was becoming childish. Indignant at this treatment, Michael Angelo would willingly have returned to Florence, and Giorgio urged him to do so. But he felt he was getting old, having already reached the age of eighty-one, and he wrote to Vasari saying he knew he was at the end of his life, as it were in the twenty-fourth hour, and that no thought arose in his mind on which death was not carved. He sent also a sonnet, by which it may be seen that his mind was turning more and more towards God, and away from the cares of his art. Duke Cosimo also commanded

Vasari to encourage him to return to his native
place ; but though his will was ready, his infirmity of
body kept him in Rome.

Many of his friends, seeing that the work at
S. Peter's proceeded but slowly, urged him at least
to leave a model behind him. He was for many
months undecided about it, but at last he began, and
little by little made a small clay model, from which,
with the help of his plans and designs, Giovanni
Franzese made a larger one of wood.

When Pius V. became pope, he showed Michael
Angelo much favour, and employed him in many
works, particularly in making the design of a monument for the Marquis Marignano, his brother. The
work was entrusted by his Holiness to Lione Lioni,
a great friend of Michael Angelo's, and about the
same time Lione pourtrayed Michael Angelo on a
medallion, putting at his wish on the reverse a blind
man led by a dog, with the words, " Docebo iniquos
vias tuas, et impii ad te convertentur," and because
the thing pleased him much, Michael Angelo gave
him a model in wax of Hercules and Antæus. There
are only two painted portraits of Michael Angelo,
the one by Bugiardini and the other by Jacopo del
Conte, besides one in bronze by Daniello Ricciarelli,
and this one of Lione's, of which there have been so
many copies made that I have seen a great number
in Italy and elsewhere.

About a year before his death, Vasari seeing that

STUDY OF AN IDEAL HEAD. By MICHAEL ANGELO.

Michael Angelo was much shaken, prevailed upon the Pope to give orders concerning the care of him, and concerning his drawings and other things, in case anything should befal him. His nephew Lionardo desired to come to Rome that Lent, as if foreboding that Michael Angelo was near his end, and when he fell sick of a slow fever, he wrote for him to come. But the sickness increasing, in the presence of his physician and other friends, in perfect consciousness, he made his will in three words, leaving his soul in the hands of God, his body to the earth, and his goods to his nearest relations, charging his friends when passing out of this life to remember the sufferings of Jesus Christ ; and so, on the seventeenth day of February, at twenty-three o'clock of the year 1563, according to the Florentine style, which after the Roman would be 1564, he expired to go to a better life.

Michael Angelo's imagination was so perfect that, not being able to express with his hands his great and terrible conceptions, he often abandoned his works and destroyed many of them. I know that a little before his death he burnt a great number of drawings and sketches. It should appear strange to none that Michael Angelo delighted in solitude, being as it were in love with art. Nevertheless he held dear the friendship of many great and learned persons, among whom were many cardinals and bishops. The great Cardinal Ippolito de' Medici loved him much, and once having heard that Michael Angelo was greatly pleased with a Turkish horse of his, he sent it to him as a gift with ten mules' burden of hay and a servant to keep it. He loved the society of artists, and held intercourse with them; and those who say he would not teach are wrong, for he was ready to give counsel to any one who asked. But he was unfortunate with those pupils who lived in his house; for Piero Urbano was a man of talent, but would never do anything to tire himself; Antonio Mini would have done anything, but he had not a brain capable of much, and when the wax is hard you cannot get a good impression; Ascanio dalla Ripa Transone worked very hard, but nothing came of it: he spent years over a picture of which Michael Angelo had given him the drawing, but at last all the great expectations that had been formed of him went off into smoke, and I remember Michael Angelo had so much compassion for his difficulty in painting that he helped him with his own hand.

He has often said to me that he would have written something for the help of artists, but feared not being able to express in writing what he wished. But he delighted much in reading the poets, particularly Dante and Petrarca, and in making madrigals and sonnets. And he sent much, both in rhyme and prose, to the illustrious Marchioness of Pescara, of whose virtues he was greatly enamoured, and she of his. Many times she went from Viterbo to Rome to visit him, and Michael Angelo made many things for her. He delighted much in the sacred scriptures, like the good Christian he was, and held in veneration the works of Fr. Girolamo Savonarola, having heard him preach. In his manner of life he was most abstemious, being content when young with a little bread and wine while at his work, and until he had finished the Last Judgment he always waited for refreshment till the evening, when he had done his work. Though rich he lived poorly, never taking presents from any one. He took little sleep, but often at night he would rise to work, having made himself a paper cap, in the middle of which he could fix his candle, so that he could have the use of his hands. Vasari, who often saw this cap, noticed that he did not use wax candles, but candles made of goats' tallow, and so he sent him four bundles, which would be forty lbs. His servant took them to him in the evening, and when Michael Angelo refused to take them, he answered, " Sir, carrying them here has almost broken my arms, and I will not carry them back again ; but there is some thick mud before your door in which they will stand straight enough, and I will set light to them all." Upon which Michael Angelo answered, " Put them down here, then, for I will not have you playing tricks before my door." He told me that often in his youth he had slept in his clothes, too worn out with his labours to undress himself. Some have accused him of being avaricious, but they are mistaken, for he freely gave away his drawings and models and pictures, for which he might have obtained thousands of crowns. And then, as for the money earned by the sweat of his brow, by his own study and labour—can any one be called avaricious who remembered so many poor as he did, and secretly provided for the marriage of many girls, and enriched his servant Urbino? He had served him long, and once Michael Angelo asked him, " If I die what will you do ?" he answered, " I shall serve another." " Oh, poor fellow ! " answered Michael Angelo, " I will mend your poverty." And he gave him at once two thousand crowns, a gift for a Cæsar or a great Pontiff.

He had a most tenacious memory, he could remember and make use of the works of others when he had only once seen them ; while he never repeated anything of his own because he remembered all he had done. In his youth, being one evening with some painters, his friends, it was proposed that they should try who could make a figure without any drawing in it, like those things that ignorant fellows draw on the walls, and the one that could make the best should have a supper given him. He remembered having seen one of these rude drawings on a wall, and drew it as if he had it in front of him, and so surpassed all the other painters—a difficult thing for a man to do who had such knowledge of drawing.

He felt very strongly against those who had done him an injury, but he never had recourse to vengeance. His conversation was full of wisdom and gravity, mixed with clever or humorous sayings. Many of these have been noted down, and I will give some. A friend of his was once talking to him about death, and saying that he must dread it very much because he was so continually labouring in his art ; but he answered, " All that was nothing, and if life pleased us, death was a work from the hand of the same Master, and ought not to displease us." A citizen found him once at Orsanmichele in Florence, looking at the statue of S. Mark by Donatello, and asked him what he thought of it. He answered that he had never seen a more honest face, and that if S. Mark was like that, we might believe all that he had written. A painter had painted a picture in which the best thing was an ox, and some one asked why it was that the painter had made the ox more life-like than anything else ? Michael Angelo answered, "Every painter can pourtray himself well."

He took pleasure in certain men like Il Menighella, a common painter, who would come to him and get him to make a drawing for a S. Rocco or a S. Antonio, which he was to paint for some peasant. And Michael Angelo, who could hardly be persuaded to work for kings, would at once lay aside his work, and make simple designs suited to Il Menighella's wishes. He was also attached to Topolino, a stone-cutter, who fancied himself a sculptor of worth. He resided for many yeaɪ s in the mountains of Carrara for the purpose of sending marble to Michael Angelo, and he never sent a boatload without three or four roughly hewn figures of his own carving, which used to make Michael Angelo die with laughing. After he came back from Carrara he set himself to finish a Mercury which he had begun in marble, and one day, when it was nearly completed, he asked Michael Angelo to look at it and give him his opinion on it. "You are a fool," said Michael Angelo, "to try to make figures. Don't you see that this Mercury is the third part of ɑ braccio too short from the knee to the foot, that you have made him a lame dwarf ?" "Oh, that is nothing ! If that is all, I will soon remedy that." Michael Angelo laughed again at his simplicity, but when he was gone Topolino took a piece of marble, and having cut Mercury under the knees, inserted the marble, joining it neatly and giving Mercury a pair of boots, the top of which hid the join. When he showed his work to Michael Angelo he laughed again, but marvelled that igno-rant fellows like him, when driven by necessity, should be capable of doing daring things which sculptors of real worth would not think of.

Michael Angelo was a very healthy man, thin and muscular, although as a boy he was sickly. When grown up he had also two serious illnesses; nevertheless he could support any amount of fatigue. He was of middle height, wide across the shoulders, but the rest of his body in good proportion.

Certainly he was sent into the world to be an example to men of art, that they should learn from his life and from his works; and I, who have to thank God for felicity rare among men of our profession, count among my greatest blessings that I was born in the time when Michael Angelo was alive, and was counted worthy to have him for my master, and to be treated by him as a familiar friend, as every one knows.

THE END.

UNWIN BROTHERS, THE GRESHAM PRESS, CHILWORTH AND LONDON.

Lightning Source UK Ltd.
Milton Keynes UK
UKHW020957090219
336936UK00009B/1281/P